Praise for *Wedlocked*

There are many books being published today that are hailed as "daring" or "brave," but for me, there is only one book that is daring and brave: this book is Jay Ponteri's *Wedlocked*. Ponteri does not flinch; he does not cower; he offers rawness and honesty, the storm, and the eye of the storm. His long hard stare at marriage and longing, at the inner life of ideas and dreams alongside the life of platitudes and home repairs, gives us a rare and undaunting meditation on and interrogation into these lives. We want him to stay; we want him to go. We want him to have the dream and destroy it too. Essayistic, narrative, and meditative by turns, Ponteri's is a beautiful and truly courageous voice.

JENNY BOULLY, author of *The Book of Beginnings and Endings*

The great Polish poet Czesław Miłosz talked about the importance of a writer to engage with his or her shadow. That is, often a writer puts forth a kind of hero sense of the self, a sort of announcement to the world that the person you are sensing beneath the writing is essentially a nice, good person. Milosz's point was that human beings are more compli-cated than simply being nice or good and that the shadow part of us holds a rich store of truth, meaning, and in the end, understanding. So it is in Jay Ponteri's memoir, *Wedlocked*, that we find a writer engaged with his shadow, wrestling with it, losing and winning with it. This is a book that moves beyond simple individual honesty to the greater more complex honesty of human nature. It's a beautiful, sticky, bloody, sweaty, feverish book that will be hard for some people to read. Those who do, though, will find that what they have imagined is true: our romantic relationships, or relationships with the lover, with the self, with the other, are as complicated and messy and ecstatic as the human body engaged in them.

MATTHEW DICKMAN, author of *All American Poem*

In our understanding of gender, relationship, and desire – there is always another frontier of ignorance before us. In *Wedlocked*, Jay Ponteri goes into the country of marriage and masculinity in a way that is freshly honest, insightful, and tragic. Ponteri's fierce scrutiny of the degrees of separation inside union has not been performed before in this contemporary register. Bravely, he shines light on regions of the male psyche that mostly have been left in shadow. *Wedlocked* is a fascinating book that will interest all men and women who struggle in that sticky, lonely terrain between bonding and bondage.

TONY HOAGLAND, author of *What Narcissism Means to Me*, finalist for the National Book Critics Circle Award

Ponteri's story offers the contemporary reader a fresh way to contemplate our country's abiding love-hate relationship with the institution of marriage. We revere it; we chafe against it. We sin in our hearts, and our guilt depends on what the meaning of the word 'is' is. This is a new and nuanced contribution to an enduring debate. I welcome it.

ANTONYA NELSON, author of *Bound*

Jay Ponteri is a brave seeker with a capacious and conflicted heart. Equal parts confession, fantasy, meditation and rant, his deeply private memoir is fearless in its exploration of dark and uncomfortable corners in his marriage. These beautifully crafted pages shine a light on loneliness, marriage, fatherhood and how we sustain ourselves in our lives of perfect ordinariness.

NATALIE SERBER, author of *Shout Her Lovely Name*

Many recent books have been written, of course, about sex, marriage, love, men, and women. Very few if any risk the level of intimacy, candor, and rawness that Jay Ponteri's book does. Very few if any behold the husband (in all his agony) with the depth that this book does. Very few if any expose the male psyche with this book's nerve. None that I can think of is smarter about the uses of fantasy. I hugely admire *Wedlocked*.

DAVID SHIELDS, author of *Reality Hunger: A Manifesto*

Library of Congress
Cataloging-in-Publication Data

Ponteri, Jay, 1971–
Wedlocked : a memoir / Jay Ponteri.
p. cm.
ISBN 978-0-9838504-8-9

1. Ponteri, Jay, 1971- —Marriage.
2. Husbands–United States–Biog-
    raphy.
3. Husbands–Psychology.
4. Husbands–Sexual behavior.
5. Sexual fantasies.

I. Title.
HQ756.P647 2013
306.872'2092–dc23
[B]

Hawthorne Books
& Literary Arts

9   2201 Northeast 23rd Avenue
8   3rd Floor
7   Portland, Oregon 97212
6   hawthornebooks.com
5   *Form*:
4   Adam McIsaac, Bklyn, NY
3
2   Printed in China
1   Set in Paperback

For Amy and Oscar
… take my shaky hands

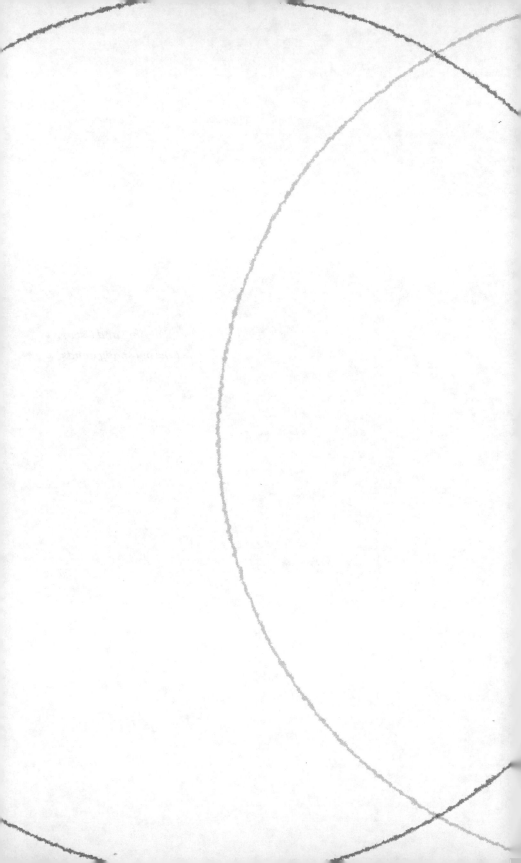

wedlocked

A Memoir
Jay Ponteri

 HAWTHORNE BOOKS & LITERARY ARTS
Portland, Oregon | MMXIII

Contents

Listen To This 13

The Manuscript (I) 19

Putt-putt 41

The Manuscript (II) 51

Lost in *Lost in Translation* 69

What's Wrong With Me 71

On Talking With Carlos 77

Man in the Bubble 81

So Hard It Bleeds 85

The Manuscript (III) 89

Tense 113

Bring In the Clown 115

The Manuscript (IV) 117

The Saddest Part of the Story 133

Before Video Games 149

The Manuscript (V) 151

The particular charm of marriage, which may grow irresistible to those who once have tasted it, is the duologue, the permanent conversation between two people who talk over everything and everyone till death breaks the record. It is this back-chat which, in the long run, makes a reciprocal equality more intoxicating than any form of servitude or domination. But for the artist it may prove dangerous; he is one of those who must look alone out of the window and for him to enter into the duologue, the non-stop performance of a lifetime, is a kind of exquisite dissipation which, despite the pleasure of a joint understanding of the human comedy, is likely to deprive him of those much rarer moments which are particularly his own. For this reason great artists are not always those who repose the most entire confidence in their wives (this is why second wives are sometimes best) and the relation of many an artist to his wife is apt to puzzle the spectator.

    CYRIL CONNOLLY, *The Unquiet Dead*

I want to know everything about you. So I tell you everything about myself.

    AMY HEMPEL, *Tumble Home*

I
Can-
not
accord
sympathy
to
those
who
do
not
recognize
The human crisis.
JACK SPICER, "Love Poems"

Listen To This

IN BED MY WIFE SAID, —I TALKED TO X ON THE PHONE. She's dating a married man. —That's what they call it, I said, dating? —They work together. —Work together? I asked, What kind of work is that? —Listen to this, my wife said, X received a text message from him, suggesting they meet for coffee and X replied, saying, *Yes, let's*, and then she got a text back, asking, *How about monkey sex?* She texted back, saying, *Even better.* An hour later she sat in a café, repeatedly checking her cellphone for the time (her married man was never late) or for texts pertaining to his whereabouts. My wife said, —Knowing X she was probably drinking a no-foam skinny latte through a straw to keep her teeth from staining yellow. That's just the kind of thing X does, my wife said. What X didn't know was that the married man's wife, using her husband's phone, had sent the text message to X and after the wife heard back from X (*Even better*), she called her lawyer who within the hour served divorce papers to the married man at his therapy appointment (as X wiped a dripped milk drop from her chin). The married man sat in the waiting room outside of his therapist's office, searching for his cellphone, first checking his pants pockets and then his laptop case and not finding it, realizing he needed to call X right away to tell her *not to dial* his cell number just in case when the door clicked open and in walked a strange man carrying a manila folder which held a divorce subpoena. I did not believe divorce papers could be drawn up and served so quickly but I did not say a thing, did not stop my wife who spoke in a plaintive, gossipy voice, as if she wanted me not so much to condemn the dalliance (my wife *would* like that but knows I'm not the type to condemn anybody for aberrant behavior) as to express the proper amount of distress over the trouble X and this married man have caused his family, i.e. the wife and daughter, himself, too. And let's not forget about X's despair at having placed herself in the middle of this family's unraveling. Perhaps my wife intended to stir up some talk about our marriage or maybe she wanted to feel my love or simply didn't want to feel my ambivalence. What intrigued me initially–and I didn't say this to my wife–was the swift course of action taken by the wife. She'd probably sneaked a peak at her husband's cell-phone record, noted the unusual amount of dialed, received, and missed calls he'd made to a certain number, or maybe she'd been suspicious of her husband already and not because of the frequency of overnight trips to Fort Wayne or the hours spent at the office on weekends but because of his new membership to 24-Hour Fitness or the way he'd telephone his wife to ask her not what or how she was doing but where she was. He shaved every morning and every morning he left the house on time, never run-ning even a minute or two late, so on the morning he forgot his cellphone his wife had listened to the saved messages from X– saved because at night amidst his family's evening rituals, e.g., playing dolls with his daughter, reading to her, eating dinner with his wife and daughter, frank, tedious discussions about the calendar and bills due soon and how his wife was keeping an ap-pointment to dye her hair the next evening so needed him home by 5:30, no later, not a single minute, he liked to slip down to the basement (I'*m going to see if the clothes are dry yet*) and listen to those saved messages, to hear X's grainy voice saying she loved him, she carried his heart, couldn't wait to apply the mouth-fuck, and while one part of him listened to these messages in the basement (*Let's sit in our booth next time*), another part of him was keenly aware (profoundly aware!) of his wife sitting at her desk in the extra bedroom, X-Acto blade in hand, halving a piece of

binder board for a journal she was making for a friend, a gift-giver
his wife, expansive in her generosity to him and their daughter
and friends and extended family and even strangers who knocked
on their door for various good causes, yet blissfully unaware
of her husband's love for another woman, for X (forever sitting in
that café waiting for the call, checking her cellphone every
minute), that same part of him aware of his daughter asleep in his
and his wife's bed, not her big girl bed, kicking off the covers
he'd pulled up just above her ear so that all he could see from the
doorway was a spray of blond hair amidst fluffy turquoise duvet.
Yet this other part of him continued to listen to X's voice while he
felt cold air leaking through the bedroom's single-paned window
(a north-facing window!), raising goose pimples on his daughter's exposed skin. He couldn't have been so dumb as to save text
messages and voicemails, he should've known better, should've
expunged all records that revealed any contact with X but
perhaps he couldn't help himself, he kept the messages because
in his mind this dalliance and the partly hidden geography it
inhabited (cafés and restaurants, stairwells, unisex bathrooms,
X's loft) were not only separate from his family but alternate,
aside from, thus impervious to the entire project of one's family,
one's real life. As if this illusory invisibility brought our dear
lovers within reach of that hidden stream upon which all of our
lives float. Adultery with its red rise of emotion and its coital
current, its identity recalibration and shared secrecy (what's more
intimate than sharing a secret from the world) voids out all
rational thought, is animal. Bouncy ball, bouncy ball. Bouncy,
bouncy ball. As if this married man's admin, his and X's co-
workers, and the barista who served them coffee each morning
didn't take notice of their dalliance, as if this married man's
wife didn't find it strange her husband drove to the convenience
store for this little thing or that, as if all of these people were
statues or furniture, as on a stage of a play no longer performed.
I didn't tell my wife that the secret X and her married man had
shared, the secret of their fucking, was the thing holding them

together, was *their love*. You deserve to understand what it feels like to love somebody enough you could die of it. Maybe while the married man showered that morning or toasted his bagel or checked his e-mail or read the *WSJ Online*, the wife retrieved his cellphone from his coat pocket. She hoped he wouldn't look for it, that on his way out the door he'd simply grab his laptop case as usual and later, her plan set in motion, she sat in the kitchen as it filled with winter's wafery sunlight; she understood yesterday morning, not this one, had been the final morning of her marriage, and last night had been the last night. She cleaned the stove. Drove her daughter to preschool. Back home she filled the feeder with seed, then sprinkled some on the ground for squirrels. What she felt couldn't be pinned down: a child running, sprinting on summer pavement. In bed with my wife I thought about this other wife's text message to X, thought about the phrase, *monkey sex*. Did the married man use those words in that order when speaking to his wife? Which is also to ask, Did the wife presume her husband might speak these worn words to another lover? Did she imagine his lips close to her ear? Somewhere in America a lonely woman thought, I wonder if my husband uses this or that phrase with his mistress or maybe he speaks from an entirely different lexicon. Or maybe this lonely woman in America thought, What does he say to his mistress about me, his wife? That I mother him, that I'm a prude because I don't scream, *Fuck me*, because I don't wail like a jungle animal. *Let's have some monkey sex, honey*, I imagine this lonely woman saying and then over the years, repeating in various tones and dialects, an actress who cannot let go of the line she once missed. Did the word monkey touch on something between the married man and his wife? I thought but did not ask my wife if she wanted me to touch her. The phrase *married man* suggests a man who cannot love another woman, a man doomed to loneliness. The designation *wife* conjures not a female spouse (or even a woman) but an entity dependent upon the presence of husband and household, a devoted book club attendee. Sweatpants and an oversized T-shirt. I think about X alone at the coffee shop, waiting for the married man with whom she didn't see herself in the future, she didn't mind he was married, it would end sooner than later but for now she enjoyed his radiant desire for her, his moist doting, enjoyed unloosening his belt buckle all the while knowing the people closest to her, i.e., her parents, best friends, sister across town, didn't know whom she was with, yes, she was closed off from the world, her hand with its middle finger raised to the collective face and it felt not good but electric and mobile, a door opening beyond her control and who knew when that door might shut. (It would, it always does.) At the café as she kept awaiting a text reply that didn't come – the time and place for monkey sex–she was sad not because she loved him but because she was no longer beloved by her married man in that moment, that tick in her short life. When he wasn't there he was away from her. In bed next to my wife, I felt for X. I wondered what it would be like to fuck X. That I didn't tell my wife.

The Manuscript (I)

I REMEMBER SPEAKING ON THE TELEPHONE LONG-DIS-
tance to a friend, a female friend. We were catching up with
each other, e.g., children birthed, books read, votes cast. My preg-
nant wife was out in the backyard, mowing the dandelions, or I
thought she was till I heard a knock at the back door, which meant
my wife was locked out and needed back in the house. Continu-
ing to speak on the telephone, I unlocked, then opened the back
door to my wife, her eyes swollen, cheeks tear-streaked, and
lips crumpled and cracked. I knew right away she'd been in our
garage-turned-studio, reading manuscript pages not meant
for her to read, manuscript pages to this very book. The work was
very rough. I had yet to make up names for secondary characters,
which is to say, the women I wrote about, the women I thought
and fantasized about or had had past relationships with weren't
named Frannie, the name of my composite character, the name
of my female ideal. I'd used actual names of real women, e.g.,
Georgia Peterson or Elaine Von Waggoner or Missy Navarro, names
familiar to my wife because they were friends, co-workers,
ex-girlfriends. Even though I write a combination of memoir and
essay, the truth is I fabricate brief instances, exaggerate dra-
matic encounters, and amplify (thus distort) discussions with my
various selves, digging for what I do not know, like I do not know
how two people can sustain a marriage over a lifetime or how
and why we give up erotic love for companionship or why, just as
I've created something meaningful and, dare I say it, healthy, I

punch the self-destruct button or why erotic love, once consum-
mated, begins to vanish or why the best sex I've ever had is in
my head. (Not that I've figured any of this out now having written
and revised the manuscript.) My wife had known I felt uncertain
about our marriage. In couples therapy, I'd told her there was
so much inside me I couldn't share with her and all of our issues
(my struggle with touch and my shameful fear of rejecting her)
seemed to press right up against this concealed inner life. What
was I dissembling? I had been thinking a lot about Frannie.
I couldn't go ten seconds without conjuring up Frannie's sullen,
hazel-freckled face. —What are you smiling about? My wife
would ask, handing me her basket of dirty laundry. —Nothing,
I'd say, recalling a disparaging comment Frannie had made
earlier in the day over coffee, the kind of bitchy prattle in which
my wife would never indulge. —A joke, I'd say to my wife, —One
I heard at work. No, I had not initiated any extramarital touch
but each afternoon I'd visit the café in which Frannie worked. We'd
talk about literature, music, our dogs and she'd pour me free
decaf lattes. I didn't ogle her or linger at the counter like other
men who held crushes on her yet inside I constructed a beautifully blistering alternate reality in which Frannie and I muddled
around together like teen lovers, broken, lascivious, uncom-
fortably confessional, unapologetically unhealthy, a life of coffee,
cigarettes, and gravy fries. Mine and Frannie's friendship in
reality helped me to populate my capacious and insatiable fantasy
life with players and situations, and the loneliness and sadness
engendered by such dreams became the manuscript's raw material. I wrote about imagining my wife's death and letting Frannie
console me. I wrote about my proclivity to sit in cafés dreaming
up varying scenarios of meeting women. Certainly one could
argue the book, that is, the manuscript taken in its entirety, is a
single, sustained dream of the other but that would be reduc-
ing the work because it's about other things too and honestly the
writer is not the best person to say what his book is about.
The point is the women in my fantasies had drastically different

personalities than my wife. Of course there were other daydreams
about which I did not write: a first kiss on the steps of a church
in Frannie's neighborhood; a quiet, studious life in North Berkeley,
a shabby cottage amidst an unkempt and overgrown yard and
inside, unlit rooms that seem to swallow whole the yard's cool
shade, rooms with hardwoods that creak and buckle as our
shadows leap out in front of our steps, Frannie standing at our
wall of shared books, fisted hands in pockets and head tilted,
scanning spines for a title to bring with her to bed, me kneeling
before her mons pubis. What was more beautiful than the mons
pubis of the woman about whom I dreamt? Perhaps more
beautiful were her bare legs tangled in blue sheets. Her body in
repose. Mine and Frannie's life is not heavily scheduled. We do
not have a baby or pets. We do not obsess over house repairs or
lawn and garden care because we rent. We sit around and read
sad books and listen to sad records and watch sad movies and we
fuck a lot too and if we leave the house, it is for food or coffee or
a book and occasionally we ride BART into the city and we don't
stay in touch with extended family nor do we discuss 401(k)s,
drywall materials, or getting together with So-and-So for dinner.
Very romantic stuff, I admit. I didn't imagine the painful route
I'd have to take to arrive at a new relationship: screams, fist pound-
ings, door slams, the spit of our incompetence, a frosty separation followed by a soul-killing divorce and a new apartment in
which my son couldn't fall asleep, the dark hallway (bulb burnt
out) connecting his new bedroom to the living area with kitchenette and lumpy futon. Or if I imagined cheating on my wife,
did I imagine the elaborate lies and the shabby network of visible
tunnels through which adulterers must move, did I imagine
the substantial time commitment necessary to flip between *two*
relationships or the bodily exhaustion of living so close to the
heart's white knuckle or my wife's face upon finding a condom
wrapper in the basement? Which is to ask, did I imagine the
reality of adultery, that it rarely lasted? Did I imagine the chiseling
pain and unending disappointment my wife might feel after

finding out I had betrayed her? Did I imagine the indefatigable shame I might feel about my own behavior? My secret desire for Frannie seemed to fasten me to an illusory present moment, but not any foreseeable future. And of course I realized human beings were naturally inclined to share meals with other human beings, and yes, I enjoyed the company of my adult siblings and parents and great aunt but I wished to free myself from activity that didn't bring me the kind of pleasure I felt from solitude, beauty, and desire. I still felt like that kid tired of being dragged around by his parents on this or that errand or to that family brunch or Sunday mass or golf club. My dreams pulled me out of bed, placed one foot in front of the other, padded the lonely walls up against which my life threw me. Mine and my wife's marriage seemed to balloon with inventory. We owned a house, two dogs, a car, we shared bank accounts and credit cards and my wife scheduled nights and weekends with activities (dinner parties, movies, etc…) and now, a baby? This inventory required cataloguing, monitoring, maintenance. My wife kept a calendar on which I forgot to write down all of my important events. I needed to take the car in for an oil change and then check and reset the rat traps. My head felt overcrowded with to-dos: work, doctors' appointments, electronic bill pay, household chores, grocery lists, weekend plans, weekday plans, weeknight plans. My secret, imagined life consoled me while erasing my wife into a smooth, blank space, an empty screen on which to project more dreams. I flew to Berkeley by myself to conduct research for a story I was writing and I recall walking up Shattuck Avenue towards Black Oak Books, nurturing a Frannie dream, spotting a bungalow I liked, a ramshackle, leaning house with untended garden. This house became a reality prop with which I could now use to furnish the house I truly wanted to inhabit – the one of my dreams. Braiding the real with strands of the fantastic distorted my sense of self enough to mute the loneliness I felt. I thought, *Frannie, let's deal with overgrown myrtle next year*, or: *Is my copy of* Too Loud A Solitude *in your to-read pile*? Or:

Knock, knock.
Who's there?
Woman.
Woman Who.
Woman Whom you love.

I didn't exactly breathe complications into my fantasies, that is, in fantasy I turned away from (not towards) complexity and mystery. In fantasy the mist-filled atmosphere, the loose dress, the minimal furnishings, the scratched timbre of two voices folding into each other – it all lacked ordinariness, the accumulation of burnished years. Dried skin flaked off to reveal moist dermis vulnerable to any touch. In fantasy I was not becoming my father (and not-my-father) nor did I scratch myself or fart. Nobody was beating me up or making me watch. No sour breath or lumps in breasts or funerals I felt guilty for not attending, no car pools, no stained underpants balled up inside a dirty T-shirt or denial or awareness of said denial, no hard and cold lips on my stubbly cheeks. No broken bicycle, no empty wallet. The moment I brushed up against such mystery, the fantasy ended. I didn't understand that the elation wrought by my dreams was, at best, fleeting and at worst, intoxicating. I woke up in a bad mood for no discernible reason. The day seemed to end before it really did. A child comes upon a closet in a cold unfinished basement, dark, seemingly endless, unfathomable, and he retreats back upstairs. My dreams seemed to say, *Come to me, follow along*, but there was no place to go except away. Some images I could have never dreamt, could only attain through experience, e.g., what her face looked like when it was close to mine, her clammy skin and hair tumbling, her eyes sort of lolling beneath half-open lids, her wolfing mouth rising to mine. Meanwhile my wife, five-months preggers, dined with close friends and discussed the alien inside her body, possible names, would there be a shower, with or without those stupid games, the benefits of midwifery, ten fingers and ten toes. In other words, very real things.

KNOWING I'D LIKELY disclose my inner life to the manuscript, my wife found pages stuffed inside the Priority Mailer in which I stored them. She grew upset as she read, then began to cry. She left the garage-turned-studio to confront me, despite the fact she knew she'd be interrupting my telephone call. The door was locked, so she knocked. She stood there, sniffling, wiping away tears till I opened the door. What astonishes me as I write this is the fact I didn't get off the telephone. In that moment, as in many others to come, I betrayed my wife for another woman. I refused to be there for her when she needed me to assuage her misery and to let her know I loved her. Instead I kept speaking to a friend, a female friend for whom, admittedly, at an earlier time in my married life I'd had some feelings, but we were friends now, that is, in my inner life I thought of her as a friend. Seeing rejection on my wife's face, I should have hung up the telephone immediately. Instead I asked my friend if she could hold on a sec. Shoving the hand cradle in my back pocket, I said to my wife, —I know why you're upset, I know you were reading my manuscript pages, pages that you were not meant to read, but I haven't talked to my friend for months and we have such a hard time getting in touch with each other. I don't recall what happened next. Perhaps we experience the deepest emotional pain, the kind arising from inflicting it on others, at a level of consciousness unfathomed by memory. Did I know I was hurting my wife? No, I don't believe so because unfortunately, at that time in our marriage, I was far removed from any sense of how my behavior impacted my wife, from what she might need or not need from me. Did my wife finish mowing the yard? Did she return to our garage-turned-studio and read more of the manuscript? Only my wife knows. Leaving the back hallway, I kept chatting with my friend, but eclipsing our conversation was the fact my wife had snuck a peek into my inner life, had traced with her finger a couple routes on the fast map of my Frannie-obsession and now I'd have to fess up or lie, which would further wound my wife.

THE LOCKED BACK door on which my wife knocked opened into a narrow, rectangular room with three stairs leading up to the kitchen. Some people would call this space a *mud room*. We called it *the back hallway*. On the walls, coat pegs and metal utility shelves held our raincoats and winter coats, boots, shoes, a flashlight, plastic bags to scoop up dog poop, work gloves – all those additional layers to protect our bodies from elements, natural and unnatural, outside the house. In the back hallway, we shook off remnants of outside elements clinging to our bodies, e.g., rain, mud, sand, shreds of leaf, paint, oil, pine needles, snow, etc... We shed some of what we dragged in with us: the outside mess. We passed between a clean, closed space in to a messier, open space we called *the outdoors*. We had to traverse the back hallway, step across this threshold mediating two radically differ-ent spaces, one in which we, my family and I, inhabited and were more protected and the other in which we were more vulner-able to the forces of nature. The back hallway was part of the larger shelter yet replete with debris from the outdoors. Once outdoors I separated from my family, could spend more time inside my thoughts whereas inside my house (in from the out-doors), my roles as husband and dad made it necessary for me to live, to the best of my capabilities, outside my distracting thoughts and outside my desire for another woman. The back hallway bridged my family life to my capacious inner life. In the back hallway, I could begin or end a waking dream. The back hallway sheltered beings in transit, not beings in dwelling. That is to say, the back hallway was not a space in which one hung out, shared meals, worked at a laptop, danced or ran in place, fucked, or slept yet when my wife knocked at the locked back door and I let her inside the back hallway, the space became *a dwelling room*. One that held mine and my wife's mutually acknowledged loneliness and the revelation of our despair. The wall(s) between outside and inside seemed to collapse, leaving my wife and me disoriented, mussed, and unprotected from the detritus of my secrecy despite the fact we stood in *a covered space*. The

outdoors of my interior life began to spill all over the inside of
our house.

TRYING TO CONCEAL my anxiety, I mean, God forbid my friend
knew my wife and I struggled, more precisely stated, I struggled
to reciprocate my wife's love, I ended the telephone call. I clicked
the hand cradle into the charger and following my wife into the
TV room and sitting on the couch, I composed my face to appear
empathic and complicit, I steepled my hands and crossed my
legs at the knee as if attendance were about to be taken. Blame
receptor: here. Husband profligate: here. The little boy who
could do nothing right. I'm not describing my wife's face and hair
or her hands or what she did with her hands when she spoke
because at this point in our marriage I was not seeing her. She
wasn't inside of me as Frannie was. In a voice composed but
tight, I asked what pages she'd read and she said, —Enough. Not
an ideal start, I thought. I thought, I would've preferred other
words like, —I happened to glance at a couple sections, or —I read
the first section and put it down because I knew what I was
doing was wrong. I didn't intend to rebuke my wife because it was
my distance (born out of my secret dreams) that had driven
her to sneak. Maybe she yanked hair strands or gnawed at her
lower lip. I can't recall. Did she ask if I was falling in love with
another woman? Did she ask if I was still attracted to her? Can't
recall. I reassured her this thing with Frannie, which was
actually an obsession, was an escape, innocent fantasy play, the
sad, bad way I medicated. Some people drank alcohol, did drugs,
fucked other women. I dreamed up alternate worlds in which
my wife was not my wife and my house was not my house. —To
make a fair assessment, I said to my wife, —You really need to
read the entire draft, which delves into my childhood and parents
and family and college life. I said, —You need to understand
the larger context of my loneliness. And I believed what I told my
wife that day – there was this history of my loneliness. Throughout childhood, adolescence, and early adulthood I met difficulty

with self-isolation and daydream. Where there was only darkness,
I imagined myself revealed in spotlight. Like walking in the
middle of the street, thinking what a wide swath I cut. Yet I was
also tiptoeing my wife and me around the unutterable truth
I loved another woman. I was lying to the both of us. This part of
me that spoke this lie wanted, in that moment, to be a good
husband, to be the husband my wife had in mind. Those who steal
do so once they've explained to themselves what they want to
take actually belongs to them. Perhaps this period of my life about
which I write is an inventory of the various ways I explained to
myself my destructive and necessary decision to fall in love with
another woman. Knowing my wife as I think I do, I imagine in
this kind of humiliating situation she would be popping hairs out
of her scalp as she did when showing me her new grays. I can't
recall what she was doing. I wish I could ask her now – all these
years later after we broke each other, bled, mended, healed,
and scarred – if she recalls her gestures during that time but I'm
afraid to bring her back to that pain, to remind her how capable
I am of hurting her, that I'm not the husband she has in mind.
My love for my wife was absent, vanished like a memory of some
pedestrian instance, like standing in line at the grocery store
or making a doctor's appointment over the telephone. We are not
present in our lives. I reassured her nothing was going on and
that I loved her. She shouldn't even bother to look askance at
Frannie. —We're not even flirting, I said. Of course we were flirting. We'd discuss literature or music or on her breaks she'd sit at
my table and we'd work the *Times* crossword puzzle. Even though
Frannie was not at all curious about other people's tastes
(therefore refused book and music recommendations from all
customers), she allowed me to turn her on to Alice Munro's work.
We'd assign ourselves stories, then discuss (over coffee) the endless layers of one character or another or a story's unique design,
the typical Munro story layered in the way birds build out of
fragile, varied materials sturdy nests in which to nest their nestlings that would, one day as birds, build other nests in which to

nest their nestlings. Like words inside of words. Like rhythm and syncopation. Worms have five hearts. Worms like the dark. Like me Frannie enjoyed handsome, hard-covered books, their dust jackets protected in Mylar. It didn't matter to her if they were first editions, which was one difference we had, albeit a minor one (aside from the major one I was married and she wasn't), nonetheless, I gifted Frannie a couple Munro first editions and she thanked me profusely. She seemed to enjoy them, for she'd handle each book so delicately. She'd barely open the boards for fear of cracking the spine. Who knows if she has kept them. Perhaps from time to time, she passes over their spines, thinking, *Pathetic married men* or *Kind man lost in America* or *What about me?*, or perhaps she has sold them back to Powell's. By loaning her books about characters and narrators who act out of their dark hearts, I was attempting to say many things to her:

> I acted out of those same dark spaces.

> I believed she did too.

> Could she recognize me as a person who knew this about
her?

> I had the empathy to know her even further.

> I intended to gift her with the kind of sustained, soulful
pleasure that came from reading a book about what we did with
our despair.

> Could we cultivate a more intimate relationship by inhabiting together the book's more sorrowful psychic spaces?

> I didn't intend for her to return the books.

A DOTING LOVER-HUNTER I became – drawing the beloved to his nest with ornamental gifts. Except I already had a nest of which Frannie couldn't be a part. I broke off little pieces of this nest my wife and I had built and presented them to Frannie. Each bit – a book, a note scrawled on decorative stationery, a pink Pearl eraser – became an irradiating, soft shard, not only to remind Frannie of my presence in her life, I imagined, but of my trembling affection for her. I wanted her to carry it around with her or store it inside her house in a special place and then I could imagine her reading that book or folding the paper in neat squares or erasing a figure; I imagined her wrapping herself in my affection for her, and this fantasy was a structure to hold my desire for her, separate from the dwelling my wife and I inhabited. I seemed to operate under the illusion I could reach for Frannie, that I could remove a part of myself and send it off with her in the hopes she would offer me some part of herself. For some time it appeared Frannie took pleasure in my company. She'd burn CDs for me, bands she believed I would enjoy (for we were both drawn to quiet, sad music) and another day, brushing her hand over my forearm, she complimented my olive-complected skin, or we ran into each other in the Blue Room at Powell's and ended up in the café, talking about therapy and medication. I confessed to her that I wasn't sleeping at night (of course I didn't say why) and when we parted, she told me things would get better and even if they didn't, being sad was so much more interesting than not and then she hugged me, our first, and that entire next week I felt her against me, her slim hands pressed like shirt snaps against my shoulder blades.

AS MY WIFE'S body healed from childbirth, we held off from having sex, and I became very horny. My wife, by the way, despises that word. *Horny*. She says it conjures up in her mind a 16-year-old boy masturbating into a tube sock. I smirk or shake my head as if in full agreement, yet most men, me included, devolve into horny 16-year-old boys (who may as well toss off into a tube sock) the moment they, we, see a woman who attracts us. In bed I'd say salacious things to my wife, like, —I can't wait to fuck, or —I want to make you come and then brush my fingers over the crotch of her underpants or tickle the skin underneath her breasts or comb my fingertip over her eyebrows, but her body was still in pain from childbirth, not ready to hold my penis in any sort of pleasurable way. Plus my prickly touch, my concupiscent speech, all of it placed pressure on my wife to satisfy me in the ways I dreamed about Frannie satisfying me in the pages of my manuscript. Those rough pages full of my secret desires and rebukes had seeped into the fabric of our real lives so that my wife no longer saw in her mind's eye her own solid self. No, she closed her eyelids and Frannie's face, open lips thick like cream, appeared in my wife's consciousness. My wife must have felt herself disappearing. In bed she'd say, —I feel so dumb, so duped. I feel rejected the second you touch me. She'd say, —If it were simply a matter of sexual acrobatics, we could take one of those yoni courses but those were real goddamn feelings you had for her. She'd say, —Let's just fuck. Or she'd shudder at my touch. My repulsion for her had spread to her or better said, my lack of feeling for her had taken root inside of her body. What she felt as I touched her was my resistance to her. Her leg or arm would seize up as if startled or cramped or she'd flinch or bat away my hand. It took a long time for my wife to get excited. She'd get real pissy, thinking about some of the things I'd written (e.g., *I imagine Frannie: heavy boobs, blue-white skin, oily black pubic hair*; Or: *every time my wife leaves the house for an errand or to meet a friend I masturbate to a fantasy of Frannie*). Or in bed my wife wouldn't touch me at all: not on the face, arms, hips, or the back of the neck. She was like an inflatable sex-toy doll and I was her lonely man. At some point my wife ceased initiating sex. I'd have to guilt her into it. —We haven't had sex for three weeks. Or in a more defeated, self-pitying tone: —You never want to have sex with me. I didn't say, —Thankfully I masturbated while you and our son were at the grocery store. I didn't say, —Maybe your body, which has just experienced the traumatic experience of pregnancy, then childbirth, needs time to heal, to return to its former sex-spear state, or perhaps your body is changing as mine is, my second chin, and gut, all that flatulence under the duvet, the onset of adult acne. I didn't say, —Let's grieve this youth-loss together. I didn't hold her. OK, I realize, reading over these sentences, my wife, upon reading this manuscript (which she has not read – I repeat, she has not read this manuscript) might feel exposed, like, *My God, my husband is writing in precise detail about the problems of not only our marriage but of my body's protest to sexual touch*. She would say, *This is business I don't even like to think about let alone tell even my best friend and now my fucking disloyal, dream-fucker husband broadcasts it to the readers of America*. I get that, but this silence about marriage in our culture is hurting so many of us (spouses, children, parents, pets, friends), leaving us alone and blame-filled. We are not so good at marriage, America. Let's flip the rickety table on its side, let's kneel down and rub ourselves in the syrup of each other's flaws and fears. Let's speak from our hearts, then let's fuck. Let's pick through the remains and find evidence of our lives. Let's make a single map of our varied hearts. Let's say, I stay up at night ticking off the women my wife cannot be. Let's say, I don't remember what it felt like to love my wife. Let's offer mandatory courses to young couples like *Sharing Bank Accounts Reveals Unhealthy Spending Habits* or *Love as Identity* or *He Said In One Room And She Said In Another Room* or *Get Married In Your 20s And Agree to Finish Growing Up Together*. Or *When Making Love Becomes Fucking*. Or *You Will Still Die Alone*. Let's shatter the opaque glass, let's squeeze the shards into a juice and drink it from the leaking cups of our bare hands.

ONE OF OUR problems was the way I put my wife in the role of caretaker and how, in turn, she filled that role. My wife was a generous, often selfless woman, devoted not only to me but to her son, her friends, our extended families, even complete strangers. She stayed in touch with many people from various parts of her life. She gardened every weekend, or when it rained, she knitted, and never something for herself, always a scarf or hat for me or a sweater for our son or a dress for our niece. She kept a leash in the car in case she saw a stray dog trotting on the street or the highway. Thank-you notes and birthday cards always arrived on time and she presented small, useful gifts to the host or hostess. She contributed regularly to her 401(k). Saw her

dentist and ob-gyn routinely, exercised, ate plenty of leafy greens
and fish and turned down dessert here and there. I, on the other
hand, was a depressive and had trouble handling the most basic
of tasks. I failed to keep track of my personal finances (always
overdrawing on my account), forgot to pay parking tickets (which
resulted in the State of Oregon garnishing my wages, thus
throwing off our monthly budget), didn't write down my appointments on the family calendar, didn't care to wash or service
our cars or bikes till they stopped working. I pretty much ceased
answering the telephone and checking voicemail. Most of the
things she did do I didn't. I enjoyed brief stints of exercise only
when I reached the point at which my body disgusted me. I
smoked cigarettes, drank coffee throughout the day and into the
night (—That's not good sleep hygiene, Love), ate way too much
bread and cereal and potato chips. Sometimes I couldn't stop
shoving food in my mouth, and it was no secret I enjoyed smoking
a joint here and there. In Amy Hempel's novella *Tumble Home*,
the clinically depressed narrator says (paraphrasing here)
depression is like having a whole other full-time job you have to
do before you can do the full-time job you're supposed to do.
You can imagine what happened: my wife not only picked up
household matters I neglected (e.g., checking messages, picking
up supplies for our son's school project, calling the cable company) but also cared for me when I refused to, as if she were mom.
I often had days, entire weeks really, when I felt a deep sadness
and moved about my day like a zombie: this despair was a burst-
ing, stifling heat pressing against the inside of my skull and the
backs of my eyeballs, distracting me from everything to which I
needed to pay attention: wife, son, the dogs, my work, and if
work was busy or if we had out-of-town guests back-to-back weekends, I became easily overwhelmed, irritable, largely absent
from the present moment and my wife, who knew my behavior
better than anybody and who, unlike me, was closely attuned
to her surroundings, felt my vacancy (my febrile inward gaze), saw
the way my bottom lip curled in or heard my teeth gnashing and

asked if we should check in or if I'd taken my medication or she
recommended a change in diet or more exercise, and even
though her recommendations might help me feel better, I grew
angry at her, for I preferred she acknowledge my sadness
without feeling like she should help me get rid of it, or I preferred
she simply ignore me completely. I told her this and for a few
weeks she worked hard to give me some space but then we fell
back into old habits. I caught a cold (smoking cigarettes depleted
my immune system so I often got sick) and she mothered me
(—I set out some vitamin C and echinacea on the counter,
or: —Maybe you should cut down on the cigarettes). I definitely
complicated matters further when my self-neglect and my
costly, damaging impulses positioned her to stabilize a situation
gone awry, like the time I ran up our credit card a few thousand
dollars (bibliophile) or when I knowingly didn't renew my medication prescription and ran out and later, suffering symptoms of
withdrawal (nightmares, hallucinations, massive headaches), my
wife had to drive me to the emergency room, and later while I
dosed up on medication and fell asleep in an ER cubicle, she stood
in a long line at the pharmacy for my prescription refill. My wife
could have been caring for herself or our son but instead spent an
inordinate amount of time trying to fix me, and that didn't even
account for the mental and emotional energy she expended
worrying about my health and the heaping ways it affected our
family. I believed she'd be much better off without me and
when I said this to her, she got sad and tried to soothe me. Amidst
her feelings of sorrow, she could reach out to me, whereas on
my best days it was a struggle for me to reach out to her. Her devotion to me seemed to arise from her soul thus wasn't easily
restrained let alone extinguished. Still I was repelled by her preen-
ing. How could my wife possibly feel sexual desire for a sickly
boy she was endlessly nursing back to health? My wife and I had
a radically different sense of what it meant to take care. That is,
what I thought was healthful often seemed to my wife like self-
destructive behavior. The other day I decided to ride my bike to

the library to return my overdue books. Pulling my cruiser from the shed in the backyard, I congratulated myself on my decision to exercise. I anticipated the endorphin buzz and salty sweat pouring from my skin pores. This ride was about 20 blocks down a street with little traffic, so I didn't feel it necessary to wear my helmet, and as I mounted my bike, my wife, outside in the garden with our son, asked me where my helmet was and we quarreled. I didn't tell her wearing my helmet felt as if I were inserting my head into a tiny, locked cage because that would not at all appeal to her way of being in this world, which is to say, she had faith one's careful decisions in this life could yield some meaning and joy, to self and to the larger community. My way of being was steeped in uncertainty and self-consciousness. For I saw all the little broken things. I often felt I was caring for me, but my wife felt differently and began to advocate for me to practice the kind of self-care in which she engaged, or when I did actually care for me at the level she did, she complimented me or hugged me and it felt like this compliment was coming from mom whose job it had been to teach me decent self-care. My point being it was not my wife's job. Perhaps my depression helped my wife fulfill a need she had to heal the sick child, which she'd possibly gleaned from her mom, also a generous, loving soul, and maybe I had married my wife because I felt at an unconscious level I needed somebody like mom to care for me, yet these needs we had, by-products from childhood, occluded other, more necessary needs, adult needs, like sexual desire and an equitable and emotional companionship. It's as if we were kids playing house, mimicking our parents' unhealthy behaviors who were mimicking their parents' unhealthy behaviors. Perhaps a more generous reading of Freud suggests not so much that us boys want to fuck women like our mothers (say, who have similar personalities) but that a boy's relationship to his mother provides a tableau for intimacy he attempts to reconstruct his entire life. That is to say, us boys, now men try to reclaim not so much the same intimacy but an intimacy that is kindred or like in nature, analogous to our origins. Do we want to be smothered with kisses the moment we walk in the door or do we want a colder touch or do we want to have to reach for what we desire? Do we want to be coddled or punished? Mom was selfless, took great care of me but her care aesthetic was different than my wife's. Mom's was reticent, less doting. Even as adults mom and I write *I love you* on birthday and Christmas cards yet we never speak those words aloud. In the moment, we stop short of feeling, as if feeling were a deep well into which neither of us want to fall and in that way mine and mom's touch is there (for we look down into this well together?) but colder and more distant. Perhaps I did want mom but was not getting mom with my wife. I do think it false to say mine and my wife's relationship didn't fulfill some of our adult needs – it occasionally did – we were kind (and enjoyed being kind) to each other and we had sex, although I doubt either of us would say our sex life was satisfying, and we took pleasure in raising our son, so, yes, our relationship had many layers, some meaningful and pliable and others thinly stretched and about to snap, but its foundation (that flimsy, barely built structure) seemed carved out of those unhealthy roles – me miserable and barely afloat and her suited up and diving in, pulling me from dangerous waters. Perhaps I needed to swim to safety on my own. Perhaps I needed to drown a little as she, dry on the dock and terrified, watched or walked away.

EVEN THOUGH FRANNIE proclaimed, over coffee or emails, how much she loved her boyfriend, we became confidants, the close, tell-all variety to which lovers aspire but so rarely form. Her break-up, my loneliness, her nowhere job with shitty customers (Vente-skinny-mocha-latte-no-whip-lite-foam), my students, her new-boy ebullience. It was so easy for me to confide to a person separate from my daily existence. We were not so cozily positioned to easily (and frequently) help or hurt each other. At a certain distance, we could admit to each other our various and separate trespasses against others, could safely accept

ourselves and each other as flawed or fucked up. We could be
more human and humane with each other.

FRANNIE IS A composite. Frannie is every girl my wife is not.
Frannie is the other woman I draw into my fantasy world, every
woman to which I masturbate, every woman I ogle, every woman
I flirt with, every woman I contrive to run into surreptitiously;
the woman on floor 19 with whom I sometimes share an elevator;
the clerk at Videorama. Frannie is a dear friend from graduate
school. Frannie is an executive assistant on 20, a barista at the
café, mine and my wife's best friend. A bookseller in the Blue
Room at Powell's. Frannie rides the number 8 bus through northeast Portland. Frannie lives three houses down from me, across
the street and two houses down, in the house caddy corner from
the playground. The one who walks her black lab by the house
around noon. An early dustjacket photograph of Alice Munro circa
1969. A student I drove home after class, a former student I run
into at the grocery store, another who signs her emails, *Miss you*.
Frannie is Salinger's Franny, obsessively in love, confused, tired,
unraveling. A thatch of red pubic hair bristling beneath. Shaven
pubis. Sinkhole. Frannie broods, is quiet, the shy one who in high
school ate in the science teacher's classroom. Frannie smokes,
Frannie shoots, pops, locks, she misses calls, avoids voicemails,
she pales in comparison, is fraught and fried and looking for a
better book to read. Once suicidal, now fully medicated, an ama-
teur expert of SSRIs, an ordinary depressive. Her soul is broken
like mine. A stolen milk crate in which I store my lonely feelings.

MY WIFE REACHED out for my hand and I shook it off. I pushed
her hand away from me. I would not hold her hand. I didn't want
to. I batted it away! Seamlessly attached to an arm end, a hand
seems like a smallish pillow out of which grows even tinier
pillows, tentacle-like and wiggly. Sometimes I want to snack on
the cartilage of my fingers! I do not intend to lay all the blame on
my wife, I want to show you what I cannot show her. I'll show you

mine if you show me yours. Guess in which hand behind my
back I hold my inside skin. In a shut fist I hold a crumpled picture
of self, *the portrait of self alone*, the epitome of my sadness that
beams black into black or it turns a blinding golden light at the
sun. Sadness is *Summer Baby*. Sadness is N O to everything and
everyone. My wife tried to hold my hand, I swatted it away. Fingers
from the same hand move independently of one another. You
little wrigglers! Our love was tired, our love was not enough, it was
petering out, was devoid of passion. Ours was the love of distance, the love of the train we continued to miss. Each clause
running into the next reveals a portrait of self alone. I mean, we
weren't so much vacationing in Jamaica but with Jamaica.
Guess in which hand I hold behind my back nothing. These
buckets with attachable claws can reach, clasp, and possess. They
are the ultimate in catch-and-release. What I thought were two
lovers making out was a woman with her back to me, rubbing her
eyes with the butts of her palms. One's fists fit so imprecisely
into one's ocular cavities. A friend described me as *not my usual
self*. We have stopped building modestly. On a street in Kingston,
I walked ten or fifteen feet ahead of my wife. I know it was not
abnormal for marrieds to walk away from each other like this, but
my concern (our concern) was the choked-to-the-point-of-
impassable path back to each other. Let's get the band back
together. Once away / always away. Once / away I stay. Ask me how
many hours per week I spent away from my house. My wife
reached for her husband, touched only the husband shell. 70
hours. That scraping noise was the sound of our death. My wife's
hands were thin and pale and tiny, a child's hands, and they
tend to run cold, and I refused to warm them. How could I shoo
away my wife's hand? How could I let her hand freeze? Our
extremities – *extreme mitts* – exist at the outer edges of our bodies,
connected to and at a distance from our vital organs. Our only
hope for relief was to walk back to our hotel, but to do so we had
to make our way through throngs of Jamaicans. I refused to hold
her hand. Upset and nervous, my wife took my hand so as not to

lose me. When held, my hand felt confined, locked up, not free, somewhere it didn't want to be, wanted to shake itself free, to move to the place of *other*, my hand felt chained to a second chain, rusted but unbreakable, chained to more chains, all of which connected to nothing I could see, to what I did not know. Guess what I hold behind my back outside your field of vision. My wife grabbed my hand, she said we needed to stay together and I tired of resisting her, I was sick of feeling lonely, of pining after hands I did not and could not hold, hands that did not, could not hold mine, not real hands connected to real arms connected to a real body with a real heart and mind, but *the other* I reached for, my thoughts reached towards the hands of a figment I could not touch. I could not have you so I desired you. I desired what I could not have. I did not desire what I had. The hand is a fucking flap. The hand holds up the face. It keeps the face from falling off. What if one of us dies feeling unloved? What if nobody holds our hands as we expel our last breath? My wife grabbed my hand, she was anxious and flustered, perhaps ashamed she needed me or ashamed she needed a man who didn't need or want her, ashamed of her desire to hold the hand that didn't want to be held, ashamed she still wanted the very thing that repelled her, so it seemed as if she *wanted* me to reject her. Slips through my fingers. My butterfingers. My wife felt a child's fear of rejection, the fear of being abandoned in a crowd of strangers. I pushed her hand away, I shooed it away, I shook it off, I ripped off that flap of skin, I brought back the night followed by the day after. She took my hand and I went limp in the digits. Flaccid cock of a hand. That hand of hers held me together and I dismissed it and without anything holding me together I began to unravel. She said, —I want to hold your hand. She said, —I don't want to lose you. She said, —I don't want us to lose each other in this ridiculous crowd. She was like a little girl terribly frightened of losing her parents. Remember those first few moments of searching the crowd frantically, not seeing anybody, only unfamiliar faces, mean faces, faces that may as well be walls. We are movable walls.

—Let me take your hand, she said. —I don't want your hand. I
said that. I was pissed off, tired of our marriage, of desiring Frannie and I felt my wife's exhaustion too, her vigilant watch for
my moods (will I push her away?), the way she carried around her
fear of rejection and the accumulation of rejection she had
suffered and would suffer, how she had to set all of it aside or
arrange it just so she could simply endure ordinary life, her
job working with kids who didn't give a shit or didn't know how
to give a shit, parenting our son, enjoying friends, she had to
tamp down the rejection, tamp down her anger at *my* desire for
other women, at my sadness, that picture of me alone I refused
to give up, the sadness in my face and the way I held my face, how
it drooped unless I held it in my hands, I mean, my sadness felt
as if it were inside my face, collapsing against its backside.
I rubbed my chin or held in my hands my cheeks. I liked to touch
my sadness. I held its hand, the hand of my sadness, partly
comprised of my feeling her feeling unloved, her pain, the sorrow
of an empty hand, the hand not held. I felt her sorrow and I
wanted to fuck it, I wanted to fuck her sorrow, not hold it. I wanted
her sorrow to give me a handjob. I began to blame myself, you
shitface, you juice of douche, what a freak you are, you cannot
give your wife what she wants. She wanted to hold my hand,
wanted my fingers wrapped around hers. I shook her hand away,
no, I let her hand go, I loosened my fingers, stretched them taut,
my hand became a sharp ledge off which hers fell. Hands made to
hold other hands. Handmade. A hand fits not perfectly inside
another. A hand holds the capacity to envelop. Palm bends around
palm. Fingers clasp. Holding hands with my wife felt like being
shut inside a faceless mask. A hug: needle-nose pliers locking.
We become too practiced not at saying no but at turning away from
saying no, from saying anything but no or yes. Can I see a different picture of self? Can I tell a different story of me, of our marriage, of our family? Can I imagine something I cannot? I pushed
her away, that's what I did, that was the story of our marriage I
chose to tell myself, the story I cannot stop telling. The manuscript.

This manuscript. The picture crumpled in my fist. My fist shut tightly.

Putt-putt

THIS IS A SELF-PORTRAIT OF ME HOUSING A HOUSE NO longer a house inside of which lives a family no longer a family.

ONE DAY MOM has a husband, three sons, and a dog. Years pass and her sons and husband, one by one but not in that order, leave the house. Mom remains, and the dog stays right at mom's feet till it dies. Then mom lives in the house alone. In self-portraiture, there is artist and artist's representation of self and between, the way artist sees himself but cannot represent on canvas. That is to say, I hold a dour view of my family's situation, the situation being my family is no longer a family and when I say family, I mean *family of origin*, that is, my parents, my siblings now grown up, deceased pets, not *family of creation*, i.e., my wife, son, pets, all living together in a single house many miles away from that original house yet coated with the detritus from the first family's dissolution. Another view, more complex, even optimistic too, is dad remarries a woman he loves and by whom he feels known and loved, his sense of mystery in the world deepens inside of him by the day. He becomes a happier person, or better said, happiness visits his marriage here and there whereas happiness rarely if ever visited his marriage to mom. Mom and the dog move into a condominium, she quits smoking, leaves behind the country club life she disdained, replaces tweeds, cashmeres, and plaids with denim and cotton, earns a bachelors degree. Votes her conscience. On a probate officer's salary, she

can barely make ends meet yet the money she has is hers. Snap.
No more banal job speak or dinner parties with mouth-gaping,
bejeweled strangers; no more bad-breath sex. No more no-mores.
My parents get along famously living apart. That's not the saddest part of the story. Also not the saddest part is mom's condo's
present state of deterioration (20 years later), a room-by-room
unbuckling, rotting floor boards underneath peeling linoleum,
faded carpeting rife with erratic depressions, wall cracks, a water
stain spreading like a spill across the ceiling, window sashes
flecked with mold spores, wood frames mushy from rotting, but
still, do not read said images of disrepair as a metaphor for
familial despair, mom is not a character in a fiction but a mom in
a condo, in America, right this moment, lying in bed asleep
or awake. She'll get to it when she gets to it. One who takes leave
leaves behind. One *leave* looking ahead, the other turned around.

I REMEMBER DAD arriving home late for supper. This word
supper I stopped saying, I mean, in the west we eat dinner, but
for supper in Indiana, mom baked chicken quarters in cream
sauce with thick noodles or beef stew or pasta with homemade
sauce and hand-rolled meatballs leftover from Sunday's supper,
or on nights when mom didn't feel like it, she ordered carry-
out from Rossini's. Chicago-style pizza with thick crust, saucy,
washed down with RC Cola drank from twelve-ounce, returnable
glass bottles. Just as mom called us boys to the table, the telephone would ring. Dad needed to finish up a couple tasks, and
mom said, her curt voice flimsily masking her irritation, —I'll
leave it in the oven, or —Just do the memorandums and get home,
why all the phone calls? After dinner, dad still not home, we'd
leave mom in the kitchen with a sink full of dirty dishes to rinse
and load in the dishwasher and pans soaking in warm, soapy
water. Mom never asked us to wash the dishes. Perhaps she
thought we'd slow her down or wouldn't be thorough enough or
maybe being the Reagan-era housewife she was, mom felt proprietary about her kitchen duties, about her assigned roles to care

for her children and to handle the cooking and cleaning. I mean,
am I the only person out there who wishes John Hinckley Jr.
had fired off a cleaner shot? Maybe it was out of generosity, love
for us boys, mom gifting us with the freedom not to have to
wash dishes, the gift really hers, taking pleasure in the knowledge
her boys were in the house, doing things boys do, playing *Pitfall*
on Atari or watching the Cubs game on WGN or building model
airplanes, or perhaps mom needed some time to herself with
her own thoughts. —Out, boys, out. Out of my weary thoughts,
mom said. She tired of us boys, our back-talk, piss dribbles
everywhere but in the toilet bowl. Mom's sorrow is the knowledge
she cannot protect her children from despair, physical injury, or
death. A son's sorrow is he cannot fathom how much mom suffers
or doesn't. Again, the telephone rang. Drying off her hands, not
in a hurry at all (Is that a pencil bump on my middle finger?), then
lifting the hand cradle to her ear, saying, —Where the hell are
you? Or —You say one thing and do another, or if she was already
in a mood, —Are you planning on coming home tonight? I didn't
hear this conversation, didn't hear mom clicking painted
fingernails against the countertop or see her bottled face or her
pink Izod shirt soaked with dishwater. This is a house that is
no longer a house, in a town away from which I moved as soon as
I could. Some customers flew in early from Toledo. Well, they
want a bite to eat of course and what can dad do anyway, he's VP
of Sales for Christ's sake, she damn well knows entertaining
customers is part of the job. Mom's thought is this: *they don't love
you like I do*. Dad says no later than 10. At 10 he's still not home
and us boys have retreated upstairs and downstairs to bathrooms,
to wash faces and brush teethers, or at the least we run water
over the bristles so it appears we've brushed, then to bed. We are
fast asleep when the automatic garage door engages, shaking
walls and floors, dad leaning shut the car door, a hushed click,
these noises touching our dreams of chocolate, neon light, or a
garter snake slithering into the water and then the doctor says he
must rip out my tonsils. Imagine walking through a snowy field,

your eyes drawn to the smooth blank and the blank blooming inside of your consciousness so you become the blank.

FOR CHUCK CLOSE, self-portraiture works towards self-revelation. Close says, *I feel freer to exploit myself than someone else, and to let it all hang out*. To what does the impersonal pronoun it refer in the phrase *let it all hang out*? To a blemish or a flaw. To ugliness. To characteristics we do not let hang out but do. My three-year-old son thinks by standing in the corner of his bedroom, his body folded into the wall's vertex, he becomes invisible to his mother and me. He calls this spot his blanket.

THE TIME IS 10:07 pm, mom pours a generous glass of chardonnay, retrieves her pack of menthols from a shoebox underneath the dartboard in the utility room, her preferred hiding space. Sitting down at the kitchen table, mom drinks and smokes. All the surfaces – countertops, glass doors to microwave and range ovens, stainless steel sink basins – shine like a dream of a blue light, a gas light, a light you can only see in your mind's shut eye. Mom smokes and drinks. Drinks and smokes. The dishwasher enters its final rinse cycle, emitting a low grinding sound, as mom thinks, one glass of wine and three cigarettes and John will be home. Mom thinks, *John is the name of my husband*. Mom raises her wine glass to her nose, sniffs its bouquet, as if the maitre d' would ever seek mom's approval. Always the husband's approval. Mom thinks, husbands are wounded birds beneath brush and dead leaves. Why not tell the maitre d' I'd like to sniff the fucking bouquet? *Friable*. Mom swishes wine around her mouth, swallows, and then returns the glass to the table. A marriage is *friable*. Her motions are fluid, lethargic, she's an American woman in Paris at a café in a quiet neighborhood, Pigalle or Le Marais, exhausted after an afternoon at Musée D'Orsay. A drink to wet her lips. Despite what any doctor says, despite medical research, despite some fucking facts, cigarettes calm her. The paper seems to whisper as it burns towards the filter. Skinny arms of smoke trickle out of the barrel. Years ago John quit. The smell might turn off or, at the least, distract a customer. Healthy men, John says, become men who lead. Lead what? Another glass of wine, two more cigarettes. Mom hates the word, *housewife*. It says nothing. She's a wife in a house. *House* first, then *wife*. Not wifehouse or wife of the house. She drains another glass, sucks down two more cigarettes. Lights one off the other. A fourth glass and she'll be drunk. God, what if one of the boys comes to the kitchen for a glass of water? She really feels like pitching her wine glass against the wall. Even when he's at home, he's not present. That is not the saddest part of the story. In bed dad rolls over to his side. He may as well lie asleep in a bed separate from mom's, across town or across the country or on another continent or planet, a bed in which she cannot feel his body's twists, cannot hear his teeth grinding. Their whole marriage, the interminable geography of their bed, contains two regions with distinct cultures and languages and neither dad nor mom travel well. His work, his customers, his country club. Her house, her friends who stay up too late and drink too much wine, her front yard with its tangled myrtle and hummingbird feeders. OK, she knows she picks at him unfairly. His love for the potato chip, his refusal to see an allergist, the hacking in the shower, his overworking. Underneath this picking festers her vacant desire. If that desire could speak, it would say, —Fix your gaze on me. It would ask, —Do you see I'm standing right next to you? —Our elbows nearly touch. Through rear window, beyond woods, climbs the access road to our street. Of the next ten cars to pass one will be dad's mint-green Oldsmobile. The client wanted to go out for a drink after dinner, he really had no choice in the matter because, for Christ's sake, he's VP of Sales, this *is* part of his job. Three cars cruise up the hill one after the other. They're driving too fast, probably teenagers trying to beat curfew. A high-pitched whine precedes a single yellow beam. Fucking moped. Mom understands, even pities her husband whose name is John, his standing suited and stiff-collared at his dresser, organizing his wallet,

restocking business cards, half-folding then tucking crisp bills
into his silver money clip engraved with company name, the
company no longer a company many years after the foundries
(die casting, engines, mobile homes) moved out of the rust belt
to southern states like Georgia and Alabama, then later to foreign
countries like Mexico and China, companies whose buildings
were razed long ago through implosion, on whose lots now sit
chain restaurants and big-box stores. This is a self-portrait of me
housing a house no longer a house inside of which lives a family
no longer a family. What I mean is a fucking moped is not a car.
Dad's boys will never go without as he did, dad's dad by day a
taster at a whiskey distillery and by night a couch creature and
beer drinker, dad's mom depleted from her work at Pittsburgh's
Kaufmann's Department Store. Next car might be his, with its
circular tail lights and low hum but it drives past our street, and
then 90 malevolent minutes pass as she downs glasses four
and five, polishes off the Menthols. Twenty-seven cars. Dad's car,
number 28, seems to float up the hill. It is 12:37 a.m. and mom's
anger fills the house, tendrils of cigarette smoke wrapping
around carpet follicles, climbing papered walls, slipping underneath door cracks, through floor vents, into my bedroom,
spreading over my Spider-Man bedsheets, coating my skin, her
muffled hostility swabbing my ear canals, dusting my eyelids.
If you are less inclined to believe a sensitive child, even one fast
asleep, might absorb such sadness, especially that of his mom's,
the person with whom he most identifies, maybe I should
fast-forward to the next morning, at the breakfast table mom and
dad saying very few words to each other, me noticing mom's eyes,
glassy and red, and her yellowish-brown stained index finger
and thumb. She smells like rubbed-out cigarettes. Shallow. Gutted.
Those words describe the tone of mom's voice as she asks dad
when he'll be home. Stepping out of the door to leave for work,
dad says, he'll call, his words rocks carelessly flung into a pond I
cannot see and that holds me under. I'm a little boy. My neck

itches and I feel flush underneath my flannel pajamas. The milk in my cereal is tepid, tastes sour.

AFTER MY OLDER brothers went off to college, Dad took a job in Chicago. During the week, he lived in a high-rise apartment in the Loop, and some weekends – not all – he drove back to Misha-waka. I don't remember caring he was gone, nor did I consider the possibility mom was lonely. What I remember is the house was no longer a house. The house had housed all that boy noise and now the house housed the noise of no-noise. In her bedroom, mom read, watched TV, did laundry, talked to grandma. She fretted over dad or didn't worry at all, she enjoyed dad's absence. Mom became that blank, a winter field untouched, devoid of human or animal tracks. The dog, with mom of course, lay at her feet, enjoying the occasional chest rub or ear scratch. The dog's hips were sore. Instead of a snug fit, it was a loose fit, or a partial fit. The hip bones slipped. She wanted to jump up in bed with mom, but when she tried to stand her hip buckled and she whimpered. She stayed on the floor, but if she lifted her muzzle, she could see mom's foot on the duvet. The dog had licked that foot before, it had salted her licker nicely. The main floor of the house, the floor between mom and me, we're talking about 2,000 square feet, was uninhabited family space. That is not the saddest part. I was in the basement, two floors below mom and the dog, where I read and watched TV and masturbated all the time. Using a goalie's stick given to me by my middle brother, I played air guitar. I mimicked Townshend in The Who, Page in Zeppelin, Hetfield in Metallica. Facing the sliding glass door opening into the woods, I strummed and sang to an imaginary stadium crowd. Like Townshend I'd smash my guitar, splay the strings. My hands bled. What was mom doing two floors above? No idea. I still don't know. Know what? Mom. A son doesn't know his mother but his mother knows him. When my brothers and dad left, where else was I to go but inside myself? In bed I'd scoot to the wall to create the illusion I was holed up in a tiny bunk of a tour bus, traveling America through the dark night, the engine's diesel rumble flowering in my chest.

BEGINNING IN 1983 my oldest and middle brothers left the house to attend different colleges. One went southeast, the other went northwest. I don't remember the three-plus-hour car rides, don't remember checking into dormitories or meeting the new roommates (dad likely reminding me to make eye contact as I shook a person's hand). What I remember are those sad drives back home to Mishawaka, the sharp sunlight, lilting corn stalks on the brink of harvest, my gritty teeth, the smell of manure and hay. Motoring up SR 26 or down I-94, nobody spoke, all of us, mom, dad, and I, zipped inside our private tents of loss. I'd miss listening to my brothers' stories about the restaurant in which they both worked, the record albums they turned me on to, the dirty jokes and raucous laughter I overheard sitting on the top step of stairs leading down to their basement bedrooms, their secretive adolescent worlds soon to become mine. The noise in that house abruptly disappeared. Feet pounding upstairs and downstairs, telephone ringing, froggy voices of friends, giggling girlfriends, mouths running afoul, that fucking scrotum or fucking mommy munch-er, the bands, the concerts, early Metallica, Rush, Ozzy with Randy Rhoads, Foghat, The Toledo Speedway Jam. What remained was silence louder than golf cleats pitched against sliding glass, silence louder than doors slammed shut or a light fixture shattered. Frosty pools of silence my older brothers left in their wake. A silence deafening, like a house missing its walls. This is memory fallen into the realm of imagination. I remember staying up late to watch *Friday Night Videos* or *Saturday Night Live*, knowing my brothers would arrive home around midnight, stoned, drunk, laid or not laid, smelling like cigarettes or campfire smoke and cold air, and once home they'd become boys again. They'd sit on the floor in front of the couch on which I lay and the three of us (then the two of us) would laugh at Eddie Murphy and Joe Piscopo or watch Cheap

Trick's *Dream Police*, just the three of us, before wives, kids, careers, when we were exhausted, heavy with our boy-days, ready yet unwilling to shut out the lights and go to our separate bedrooms. On the last hole at Putt-Putt Golf & Games, the ball dropped in the cup and disappeared into some place unseen.

—LEFT BALL.
—Right ball.
—Who's the penis in between us?

LATE IN THE 11th century Bohemond led an army of leather-clad crusaders into Constantinople. He'd rape and kill women and girls in front of their husbands and fathers. The young boys, he'd castrate – tying their genitalia around their father's faces like kerchiefs. Half a head taller than most men, he was built like a stone hauler, but what terrified people the most was his sickly urine-yellow hair and pasty skin. After Constantinople fell, Bohemond invented a game in which crusaders stood atop the town wall and lobbed dead Turks to the ground where his challengers stood with swords raised. Human skewers. Even the most barbarous crusader could barely hold a single dead Turk. Bohemond would skewer three, sometimes four, lifting them to the sky, to his Creator, not as an offering but as evidence of a world turned upside down. Three hundred years later Saint Louis, shameridden, taunted by his mother's oblique piety, endless disapproval bunching her bloated face in his thoughts, wore into battle underneath his armor a hair shirt made of sharp wire. I'm the youngest of three boys. Had I lived in the middle ages, dad would've either killed me or sent me to a monastery for study and silence. One can kill the same person over and over again.

The Manuscript (II)

FRANNIE ASKED A MUTUAL FRIEND OF OURS TO SHOW her where I lived, which he did after her shift had ended at dusk. I can imagine Frannie's impetus; perhaps she wanted to sort out the confusion she must have felt, that is to say, perhaps the way I continued pouring myself over her butted up against her knowledge I had this other constructed space of possible desire. Perhaps she needed to match up her own imagined picture of my married life (me on the couch reading a book or laptop on lap, emailing her or who knows what she imagined) with something actual. She needed to know I was not merely a figment roaming around the café at which she worked. It's not unlike when I hide from my son an object – a ball, an action figure – behind my back, and he sees my arms looping back around my waist but not what I hold in my hands, so I have to show him to reaffirm his knowledge that objects – a compass, a measuring tape – don't vanish just because they've moved outside one's field of perception. Or do they? I guess Frannie wanted a real close look because she and our mutual friend sneaked around the front yard and peeked in the bay window, spotting my wife and me lying next to each other on the couch like teen lovers, watching TV, *The Simpsons*. Rarely did we watch *The Simpsons*, let alone cuddle up together on the couch; usually we were in different rooms, me in bed with a book opened and my wife stretched out on the couch, knitting or listening to records. I cannot recall why my wife and I would've decided to watch TV other than maybe we had had a horrible fight earlier in the day and were now spending time together in an attempt to comfort each other, also to draw back into a less emotional space. Since this instance occurred before my wife had found the manuscript, I'm guessing (sure about this) the fight had concerned a home remodeling project (bathroom) – more specifically how the work cut into my reading time, how I disdained the work, how I'd regretted letting my wife talk me into buying a house. The truth is I don't care to own a house. Why does our culture place so much value in house ownership? After my wife and I die, everything we own becomes a nuisance for my son. We are adding tasks to our son's future to-do list. What's wrong with renting? I don't want a lot of stuff. To be fair, my wife didn't talk me into buying a house, I went along with the whole thing as if I were her child, not her discerning husband. That is, I didn't share the concerns I had about house ownership because I assumed my opinions were wrong, assumed what was right was what somebody else thought, was what not only my wife wanted but what American culture seemed to espouse. Get married. Buy a house. Procreate. I chalked up my resistance to house ownership as immaturity, another piece of evidence I was unwilling to grow up but the new-me, the writer-of-this-manuscript-me, the me who knows the grass on the other side is yellow and trod upon and patchy like thoughts, the me who understands there are many ways to live in this world and that life could end this afternoon if a bus plowed over me or if a stray bullet blasted my heart or brain, this me now knows better, knows the hours wasted sitting at the desk of some asshole mortgage broker are gone forever and if I could do that over, I know, I can't, but if I could, but why even bother with this line of regret? The next day, after the mutual friend reported all this back to me, I felt heartbroken. Frannie had been so close to my bedroom, to my books, to the bed where I fell into restful naps. To her, my wife and I likely appeared as felicitous intimates. Conversely, Frannie saw herself as *the other woman,* her nose pushed against a glass wall fogged with her own sour breath, she was the woman about whom my wife knew nothing. I imagine Frannie realized in this instant she could no longer hold still as I extended my reach towards her. A few days later up at the counter I told Frannie I had some news for her (new book forthcoming by Alice Munro), and with her voice peeved and ironic like a needle popping a balloon, she said, —You're getting a divorce. Her face with its spindly gaze and locked lips and her thumb thwacking the countertop next to the tip jar (looking empty I might add) exacerbated my feelings of profligacy. Frannie turned around and flipped a sandwich burning on the panini grill while some newbie rang me up. Her comment that day made it seem as if my attraction to her (my continued presence at the café, emails, books I gifted her) was a source of pain damaging her livelihood. Yet so oblivious (so inwardly drawn) was I that it seemed impossible Frannie have feelings for me or Frannie feel my feelings for her. I was filled with love for her yet I couldn't at all acknowledge this or the behavior arising from my feelings – that is, I couldn't see any of this as *actual*.

BEFORE MY WIFE had read my manuscript, Frannie had attended a reading I'd given at a community college. My wife attended too and yes, I was anxious that my wife and Frannie would be enclosed within the same four walls. It felt as if I were directing a play of one of my sleeping dreams in which people from disparate parts of my life gathered in a single room. These people, all played by themselves, seemed to take direction from my repressed desires. My character read aloud a story I'd written about a slovenly, self-absorbed young man who loses his dog. My wife sat mid-room, hands in lap, face attentive while in the back left corner, tight-lipped Frannie, aggressively resist-ing my eye contact, stared at her hands – more like reproached her hands, one rubbing the other á la Lady Macbeth. We seemed to all play our assigned roles: asshole man, wife in the dark, and agitated other woman. Afterwards Frannie exited stage left whereas others, wife included, hung around to compliment me or thank me for inviting them. I can imagine my wife reading that last sentence, not at all enjoying the fact that I lumped *wife* in with *others*, not enjoying the inconspicuous syntactical signals, e.g., the word *wife* tucked inside a parenthetical phrase (a mere afterthought), embedded within the already forlorn dependent clause relegated to the sentence's end, like coffee dregs or the last, weak hit off a cigarette. Later that night, Frannie emailed me telling me how much she'd enjoyed the reading and what parts of the story were her favorites. She ended with: *Sorry I couldn't tell you this to your face.* Her tone struck me as apologetic but blunt too, so what seemed left unsaid was *Sorry I couldn't be in the same room with your wife because I have feelings for you and I don't want to be hurt or hurtful* or perhaps the unsaid was I *know you have feelings for me and I have somewhat complicated feelings, scant feelings for you so don't blame me if I'm uncomfortable around your wife whom you barely discuss in my company or emails.* I wished the unsaid was *I wanted to be there with you, to see your face, to take you in.* That night I didn't sleep. I thought about Frannie, thought about how hurtful my behavior was, how Frannie felt my feelings for her. My God, did I think I was living in a bubble? Yes, I did – I lived in the bubble of my imagination.

I DO NOT remember my love for you. I do not remember dreaming about you. I do not remember the night we fell in love. I do not remember walking you to your car parked outside the tennis courts near mom's new condominium. I do not remember asking you if I could call you by your nickname, the one used by your friends. I do not remember you saying, —You use my first name. I do not remember realizing this as a good sign, that is to say, you wanted to reserve for me your *actual* name, as if you were giving you to me. I do not remember pining after your lazy brown curls. I do not remember looking at your hair and thinking, *The sea.* Thinking, *Cherry blossoms.* Thinking, *On The Road.* I do not remember calling you the next day. I do not remember feeling for the first time beneath a winter sweater your tense breasts. I do not remember loving your particular silliness, which I describe as

part-Fräulein Maria and part-Daria. I do not remember our
mutual silliness and our burgeoning love for each other assuag-
ing the despair I tried not to feel over my parents' divorce, the
despair I tried not to feel over the loss of my family of origin. I do
remember the despair I tried not to feel. I do remember trying
not to feel a combination of *Your Childhood Ends This Moment* and
Feel Ashamed Of Everything You Do Not Know. I do not remember
how my brothers and I met our future wives the year following
our parents' divorce. I do not remember running into you at Tower
Hill or the bathing suit (navy bikini) you wore or wanting to lick
the skin beneath. I remember my love for you, but do not remember what it is like to *feel* love for you. I remember the fact of
feeling but not the feeling beneath fact. I do not remember wanting to introduce you to my friends in Milwaukee. I do not remember the loneliness I felt over living in separate states. I do not
remember feeling hurt that I could not touch you when I wanted
to touch you. I do not remember dreaming the two of us together.
I do not remember my deep appreciation for your intelligence
or for the art you made. I do not remember the giant sculpture of
a hitchhiking thumb. I do not remember the book of Tom Clark
poems you gifted to me for my 20th birthday. I do not remember
making mixed tapes for you or the hours we spent speaking long
distance over the telephone nor do I recall listening through
headphones to The Replacements song "Can't Hardly Wait" on
the train ride from Milwaukee to West Lafayette. I do not remember *play-stop-rewind-play*. I do not remember our sloppy post-
adolescent adolescent sex. I do not remember making you come
for the first time at a hostel in Barcelona or going down on you
in mom's condo. I do not remember thinking, *I want to marry you.*
I do remember not thinking, *I want to spend the rest of my life
with you.* I do remember not thinking, *The rest of my life is an impossible time to fathom let alone plan for or commit to.* We lose
memory of feeling. Our psychic state (at this present moment of
composition) gives rise to particular memory. Memory falls into
the realm of imagination. Like I remember falling in love with a

woman who lived in my dorm and falling out of love with you like one flips a switch, extinguishing yellow lamplight. I remember not having the courage to tell you I did not love you. I remember hanging out with you over Xmas break and you wanting to fool around with me even though our relationship, our love for each other, was fading (or had faded) and me not wanting to touch you, not capable, too ashamed of casual sex, too ashamed I was hurting you. I remember thinking my touch hurt you. I remember telling mom at her no-longer-new condo you and I didn't seem to fit together, as if my passion for literature and art and music and my anger at *All Things Dad* precluded silliness and potential for meaningful, intimate (or even casual) connection. I remember raising my middle finger to all establishment and tradition that didn't match up with my punk effrontery. Fuck the church, fuck khaki pants, fuck marriage, fuck the music of the Grateful Dead and Jimmy Buffett, fuck the upper class and the upper-middle class, fuck university administration, fuck the Bush administration, fuck the war in the Gulf. I remember being 21 years old and everything having to match up. (Nothing matches up.) I remember wanting stormy weather and high moods. I remember, in other words, the pictures of me alone. I do not remember dreaming of your springy curls. I do not remember dating a woman who broke up with me because she felt I was still in love with you. I do not remember standing next to a tapped keg, telling you I loved you. I do not remember what it feels like to feel love for you, that feeling an opening for you to pass through and step into this picture of me, like the feeling of two lovers whispering to each other, the content of which only they know, the feeling of *We Are The Only Two Remaining In The World*. I had those feelings for you but do not remember what the feelings feel like. I do not remember childlike wonder lacing up a pair of *pure desires*. I do not remember that rare readiness to receive anything and everything from the other. The other who is *actual*. I do not remember seeing Nirvana at the Aragon *Brawl-room* in Chicago a few months before Kurt Cobain shot himself

with a shotgun. I do not remember staring at the snapshot of the
two of us in Pamplona, although I do remember leaving you
at the train station. I remember feeling relieved, I could be alone
again, I could separate myself from the shame I felt over rejecting you. I remember feeling sad too, that feeling of sadness like
walking home from a minimum-wage retail job in heavy rain,
listening through headphones to Elliott Smith. I remember enjoying that sadness, that deluge, calling it, *My New Home*. I remember not being able to articulate why I felt sad. Was I sad because
we couldn't stay away from each other? Was I sad because I wanted
to fuck you without loving you? Was I sad because I couldn't NOT
reject you or anybody who knew me as my brothers and parents
knew me? Waiting for our separate trains to pull into the little
station at Pamplona, I went inside the bathroom to find a Span-
iard passed out (drunk?) across the tiled floor surrounded by
human feces. I remember the smell of human feces. Pissing in the
urinal overflowing with vomit, it felt as if I were eating my
insides. I do not remember repeatedly staring at the snapshot of
the two of us in Pamplona. I do not remember my desire for you
catching fire and warming me against the cold of my seemingly
endless feeling of loneliness. I do not remember staring at that
photo. I do not remember looking at your tight curls and thinking,
Rainbow lollipop. I do not remember watching Kurt Cobain grow
impatient as he tried to figure out whatever sound problem he was
having with his beautifully beat-up Fender Jazzmaster. I do not
remember thinking, *To destroy is to create*. I do not remember
thinking, *Fuck you, keep it out of my face*. I do not recall the orgasm
to which I brought you in Barcelona, do not recall how your
small panties fit so snugly on your pelvis. I remember disagreeing
with you in Barcelona. I remember us walking around Barcelona, stoned, drunk, and fighting about nothing. I remember disagreeing with everything you said. I remember wanting to say,
Who You Are Is Not OK. I do not recall, later that night, slowly, hesi-
tantly, sliding my hand in seemingly docile increments towards
your thigh, then against it, on it, around it, as if I were too ashamed

to say, *I Want to Fuck You*, too ashamed (and too young) to say, *We May Disagree But We Keep Reaching For Each Other*, too ashamed I desired you without loving you, or too ashamed I desired you without knowing I loved you. I do not remember feeling love muted by anger. I do not remember Kurt Cobain yelling at Chicago fans for booing him and his inability to figure out whatever sound problems he was having. I do not remember taking the snapshot of the two of us in Pamplona to Kinko's to make a color copy of it. I do not remember including the color copy in a letter I wrote to you. I do not remember my love for you snapping words and phrases into place. I do not remember pouring myself over you. I do not remember Kurt Cobain fed-up with the audience in Chicago booing him, walking offstage long before Nirvana's set was finished. I do not remember my love for you. I do not remember what my love for you feels like. Did I think about you every moment of the day? Could I not get out of my thoughts the image of the ringlets of your hair, your blue eyes, and your stalk neck? What does it mean for our marriage that I do not remember what it feels like to love you? What lies beneath what I do and do not remember? Are memories like empty corn husks or shells tossed to the floor? Are memories what remains after we spend ourselves? I do not remember the audience in Chicago booing Kurt Cobain long after he walked offstage. I do not remember my flight descending into Chicago, towards Midway Airport. I do not remember Kurt Cobain running back onstage and leaping into the hands of those same fans who booed him. I do not remember Kurt Cobain letting the same people who ridiculed him carry his weary, heroin-addled body. Why can't we let others carry us? Why is it so difficult to let, if only for a moment or two, the people who love us carry us? I do not remember looking out the tiny oval window of the airplane at Chicago spread out before me, the lights at night arranged in beautifully imperfect grids, gleaming and signaling and running like a suicide into the inky-black blob of Lake Michigan. I do not remember my desire, my anticipation for seeing you. I do not remember floating in the humid ether of the possibility you still loved me. I do not remember my reaching for you. I do not remember tousling your soft curls around my finger, moving my lips close to your face, and whispering in your ear. Was it the left ear or the right? I do not remember. I do not remember my reaching as a picture of me with you. I do not remember driving around Tucson late at night with the windows rolled down listening to Yo La Tengo's "I Can Hear The Heart Beating As One." I do remember the picture of me alone, I do re-member dad alone in his high-rise apartment, I do remember mom alone in her new condo. (I do not remember that they are not alone.) I do not remember the train ride back home to North-ern Indiana, *The Region*, the South Shore train taking me to you. I do not remember the blighted gray streets of Gary and Michigan City lined with ramshackle homes by which the train passed. I do not remember leaning porches and weathered paint. I do not remember frozen white fields stretching towards the burnished horizon of bare trees. The entrance to the Northern Woods. I do not remember Kurt Cobain floating atop the audience of Chicago, letting those who booed him carry him, as if he could save us from our own anger and loneliness. I remember you, not the feel-ing of loving you, not the feeling of you.

FERNANDO PESSOA IN *The Book of Disquiet* refers to the world outside the self as *in life*, which suggests the world of self, i.e., living inside one's head (one's thoughts, dreams, memories) is somehow *outside of* life, yet it seems imprecise to identify this interior state as *in death*. Perhaps I mean to say, *somewhere in between life and death*. Sometimes I can remember a gesture or action if I first remember what thoughts passed through my mind at that instance. Perhaps living inside one's head is the slow construction of the bridge on which we travel towards death – that is, we pass through ourselves towards death. Whereas the exterior world, the landscape outside of me, my house, job, family, and neighborhood, is mute, without mystery, devoid of doors and windows that look out onto the world even though that's exactly where I am, as if I cannot see what lies in front of me even when I plead with myself to look, you motherfucker, look at your wife, look at your son. But when I do involve others in my life, I leave open the possibility (the inevitability) I might leave them. Often but not always I identify myself as somebody who fails at most things.

I TRIED TO make eye contact, to catch Frannie's gaze, to carve out an erotically charged play space (to acknowledge we were animals free to fuck) yet when she did meet my gaze, I averted my eyes, not out of shyness but shame, the self-shrinking me vanishing from the present moment the way a kid played *invisible* to evade a scolding. Sitting at the café, I retreated inside my thoughts. I attempted to remove myself from time. I died a little here. I could not help but swarm her, clicking mental snapshots to furnish my dreams of her (dreams of that elusive other) that held at bay the loneliness I felt. Oddly enough in my dreams I could never know myself as I was, as a husband and now a father and an artist. Memory: mom asking my older brothers to play with me and me weighing my desire to play with them against the guilt I felt from keeping them from what they wanted. I suppose most heterosexual men enjoy gazing upon face and hair, buttocks, breasts, and legs. But each man, I believe, carries his own particular anatomical foci. The way hair spreads over bare shoulders. That skin sliver between shirt and pants that flashes like a discarded gum wrapper on a sidewalk. Neat breasts pressed into a close-fitting camisole. If you say the word *nipple* around my friend D, he closes his eyes and sighs deeply. Sloped cheeks, green eyes. Nose. Freckled, pale legs spill out of a miniskirt. Sandals hang from feet with freshly painted toes. Dip a single toe in cold water and your entire body shivers. To be full of something that is yours and not yours and nobody else's.

IN BED I would say, —Let's have sex, not tonight, but say, Tuesday night. The heads-up gave my wife time to mentally prepare for my touch. When we did fuck, she'd become angry. She'd straddle me, cuff her hands around my wrists, pin me to mattress. Not out of lust. Out of a dire need to express her frustration with me, as if to say, *You rejected me so I hate you* and I'd try to free my arms from her hold so I could roll her over and lift her legs over my head like TV antennae, bracing them against my shoulders and chest, allowing me a generous view of her plaid knee socks stretched tautly over her calves and of my penis gamboling in and out of her but she'd refuse to loosen her fingers pinned to my arms and then this haunted look (distant, hurt eyes, lips sucked inside mouth) would settle over her face as if she were imagining Frannie's body in place of hers, my penis filling not my wife but Frannie and then that song would play in my wife's head by King Missile titled "Detachable Penis," something about a man detaching his troublesome penis before he leaves the house and the next morning he can't find his penis anywhere and my wife, indignant at me for losing track of my penis, my heart, my mind, would push her fingernails harder into my palms. In bed my wife said: —It's not that I don't enjoy sex when we're having it, but if I start thinking about those pages, that goddamn Manuscript, my wife said, —I feel duped all over again. I think, *he doesn't like me, why does he even try?* I think, *he just wants to fuck me.* In bed I told my wife we seemed to mistake each other for lovers. I mean, there were parts of ourselves that were missing children, without any hope of being found. There was a broken part of me drawn to sad art, to sad people. Raskolnikov, meet Holden Caulfield. Elliott Smith, meet Sylvia Plath. I did not *read lightly.* I refused to talk about the weather. If one of my limbs fell asleep, I luxuriated in its painful tingle, the delight of losing feeling. I liked losing at sports and at games, liked congratulating the winners and feeling in return their attention of camaraderie, pity, or scorn or if I did win, I felt bad for those who lost. Perhaps I felt envious. What I'm getting at is this broken part of me felt to

me unknown by my wife. She didn't always embrace my despair.
Her opinion was that depression could be treated, so why
should I live with the symptoms. I had grown used to my sadness.
I understood it as a coarse yet durable thread weaved into the
fabric of my being. When I found out one of my students had tried
(but thankfully failed) suicide, my wife's comment was, —Sounds
like a real stable one. My wife's snap judgment, her lack of
compassion upset me. This was a human being struggling with
mental illness. Maybe my wife felt my concern (let's face it, my
love) veering away from her (once again) towards some strange
woman. And wasn't all this hullabaloo about our conflicting
personalities (our loss of identity, of self inside the marriage) a
deception concealing the fact I loved another woman? Yet I can't
deny I hungered for a different kind of companionship, one more
roughshod and jackal-like. An example: my wife and I watched
the film *Elephant,* directed by Gus Van Sant, set in the very Northeast Portland neighborhood in which we lived. Picture my wife
and I lying at opposite ends of a couch under a fleece blanket
gifted to us by our parents the previous Christmas, dogs curled
like little rings in our laps while outside windblown rain lashed
against the siding and windows and later on the porch, blew over
our pink glider and antique church pew. It was the kind of night
homeless folks cocooned themselves inside soaked sleeping
bags under the Burnside bridge and prayed (or didn't) for death
or for a time blip, fast-forward to the next morning or next week
or next life. But what do I know about homeless people? Just
because I can imagine their experience doesn't mean I know
them or know what it's like for them. I do know (or think I know)
my wife doesn't like to watch violence in films or on TV, so a
shooter flick might have not been the best choice, yet I insisted on
bringing it into mine and my wife's house, our house. *Elephant*
begins by juxtaposing shots of high-school-aged students moving
through what seems like a typical school day with shots of two
outcast-boy types at one or the other's house filling a duffel bag
with automatic weapons. You the viewer know the shooting is

imminent, but these boys' schoolmates do not, which imbues their mundane gestures, routines, and rituals with an ethereal slowness. A boy and a girl cut class, saunter through empty halls holding hands; another boy photographs the teenaged couple under a tree in Fernhill Park, and later in the dark room, he gingerly dips the wet paper in chemicals; in gym class, a shy girl jogs around the outdoor track while more popular girls laugh at the jangly way her limbs move. We beat back death with ordinary gestures, Van Sant seems to say. Van Sant seems to say, Nesting inside the adolescent shell is a future adulterer and a boy once skin-and-bones becomes obese and bored with answering emails and a varsity cheerleader morphs into the young woman who prefers her thoughts and dreams and memories to the company of others and to the body of Christ while the bully now drives a truck for a bottling company and suffers from chest and neck pains. Identity is fluid and elusive, Van Sant seems to say. Van Sant seems to say, Before it's too late, look into the sky and follow the line of a single snowflake's descent. The film juxtaposes such quietly bulging instances with instances of fear and failure and desperation, the two boys, soon to be shooters, locked inside the identity-prison of Male Outcast (—*You fucking freak! You fucking Indoor Kid!*), these boys cleaning and loading weapons, playing violent video games, eating countless bowls of Cap'n Crunch, fucking in the shower. These boys with gangly arms and ribcages protuberant. The other kids know not death shall visit by day's end (and with what will you fill your last hours?) while the viewer's burden of said knowledge amplifies the existential crisis we all die alone with our fleeting thoughts, with our ghosts and phantoms, with our shameful memories, with our transient moments of brightness. Will we die next to a person who loves us? Or perhaps we will be surrounded by strangers, people we have never loved. Perhaps we sit near an acquaintance (one cubicle over or at the bus stop) and we say hellos and goodbyes and chat about restaurants or our pets but we never know each other, not really, not the obsessive material. Bird watching?

Running marathons? Masturbate-a-thon? Ballooning? *Mrs. Robinson. Would you like to see a movie?* says Benjamin. Regarding the violence of the shooting, Van Sant uses restraint. The brutality is spare and cold. Van Sant emphasizes facial gestures and sounds. Cut to an empty hallway outside the library inside which doors slam shut and kids scream as gunfire from automatic weapons strafes and swirls, boot heels clapping linoleum. Van Sant positions the viewer at the crime's terminus, the effect being that it's *about* to spill out of the screen, onto us not-so-innocent viewers. I thought it a brilliant film and afterwards I wanted to discuss with my wife Van Sant's decisions, how he shows compassion for victims and shooters, how he points no fingers at parents or Marilyn Manson or bullying kids, how Van Sant distills the event to its essence: those who shoot, those who are shot, and those of us lucky enough to survive but who must bear witness. All of us endure extended instances of loneliness, uncertainty, and anger, and we all wish for relief, for release. My wife, tossing the blanket off her lap and moping towards the kitchen, said there's nothing redeeming about the film and that she didn't want to talk about it. —Wait, I said, —Why can't we talk about it? She scooted into the bathroom. I heard water running, I heard stiff bristles on teeth. As she did calf stretches, her ankle bones popped. This was my wife's pre-bedtime routine. The phrase *bedtime routine* sounds so rigid and cracked like a chipped tooth, but it's not my wife or her routine to whom I compare a chipped tooth, it was my feelings for my wife in that moment. Question: can't an oil stain with its unlikely shape and implacable sheen, its lethargic devotion to spread across the pavement, emit a kind of industrial beauty? My wife lifted her tiptoes, then fell back on her heels, lifted then fell, all the while scrubbing her incisors. Then the click-click-click of waxless floss snapping tooth enamel. I felt lonely. I dreamt of Frannie. I tucked me and Frannie inside an old sleeping bag and held her so tight that my shoulders and hands ached. We live so many lives aside from the one we live. My wife and I shared a last name, a

last name typed- or handwritten (or stamped!) on letters and
postcards delivered by uniformed strangers to a black box
fastened to a house we owned and in which we both lived. We
seemed only to exist as recipients of other people's inquiries
and demands. Together we nursed not so much a long history
together but memories (in quick decay) of a long history,
that history too often informed by a false sense of self, that I was
alone in the world. (I wasn't.) And now we had a child, which
was, among other things, a harbinger of our respective deaths.
What kind of situation must a writer fabricate for *The New Yorker*
to print the word *Suddenly*? No matter what my wife's response
was to Van Sant's film, by that time I'd turned away from her.
It didn't matter to me that violence (human or animal) disturbed
my wife, that one more instance of under-parented children
shooting up heroin or just shooting spit wads would do her in, my
wife, an inner-city school teacher who worked with kids with
severe emotional disabilities and learning challenges, whose
parents often suffered debilitating mental illnesses and incurable
addictions. Like a shoveler of snow in Siberia. Or a cockroach
controller in New Mexico. Suffering and despair filled her work-
day, so the sad films to which I was drawn should've been out of
the question. I heard her. I understood her situation. Yet at Videorama I always chose the wrist-slitters: *Elephant*. *The Elephant
Man*. *Midnight Cowboy*. *Apocalypse Now*. *Henry Fool*. The films of
Philip Seymour Hoffman. *Love Liza*. *Happiness*. I mean, why
couldn't I do this one thing for my wife who gave so much to
others? Just grab any shitty Hollywood movie in which simple
problems of very beautiful (and boring!) people disappear when
our hero(es) make the correct choices. I cannot help myself!
My body that wanted something other than my wife couldn't help
but reach for *Elephant*. After working with people whose problems could never disappear, could only be consoled, my wife
needed me to console her, she needed simplicity, even an uplift!
At Videorama I didn't consider what my wife might want or need
and at home, five minutes, ten minutes, however long it took my

wife to realize the characters' problems were *our* problems, blistering and seemingly unsolvable, she'd begin to wring her hands or crack her knuckles and before lifting from the couch to commence her bedtime ritual she'd shake her head or swat at nothing in front of her face. I don't know why she watched *Elephant* all the way through. Maybe she was trying, for me. Perhaps the film's despair immobilized her. In bed that night, I tried to explain to my wife that telling a story devoid of hope was itself a hopeful act, especially when the emotions were rendered with precision and complexity and my wife said she disagreed. I can't recall her exact words but the message I received was this: the kind of experience to which I was drawn didn't appeal to her. She turned over to face the wall and fell asleep. Why have we stopped gazing at each other? Can we recall the exact day when one of us first looked away? I continued to seek out sad Frannie for companionship (coffee, discussions about films and literature) and in my fantasy life, we became lovers and partners, splitting cartons of cigarettes and running up credit cards. Our socks continued un-darned and new positions were rolled out. In therapy (individual), I realized all of the women over whom I obsessed in past years shared a quality of brokenness. My therapist suggested I introduce my broken self to my wife. Demand my wife to shelter this real-me. Or maybe if I showed her mine she'd show me hers. Yet did I really want my wife to shelter this real-me? Didn't I want out of my marriage? Yet it would be more difficult to leave my wife and son, to know for the rest of my life I'd broken apart the three of us. Conversely, it would be easier for me to stay in the house and slowly lose my mind, especially easier for a person like me who can't bear to hurt others (can't bear the knowledge he has inflicted pain on others) so that my feelings of loneliness would never radiate as much pain as the knowledge I'd damaged my wife and son. But wouldn't my unhappiness at home with my family give rise to a nasty resentment that would, in turn, coat both my wife and son? I think of Kenneth Koch's poem about one train hiding another like the desire to fuck another woman hiding the desire to leave my wife or the desire not to feel sad. And perhaps what hides those other desires is the act of writing this very sentence.

Lost in *Lost in Translation*

SHE SITS IN THE WINDOW SEAT, KNEES FOLDED INTO her chest, staring out at the Tokyo skyline. I've never been to Tokyo so I cannot say what exactly Charlotte sees out there. I do know she's not going anywhere today. She lights a fresh cigarette off the old. Recalls picking up her mom's porcelain doll, tracing a fingertip over its blood-colored mini-lips, then flinging it against the papered wall. Loneliness is pining after what you don't have and shutting out what you do. On the desk his lenses of zoom piled atop hotel stationery filled with her scrawl; her guide books and relaxation CDs; his Yale-blue, Sears suit coat draped over the chair over which she let him bend her not ten minutes ago; birth control pills; her notebook; white boxer shorts fecal-rubbed in the crotch. She sees nothing she wants to see, only abraded skin off which skin has been torn. I wish I could leave on the nightstand a beautiful novel but I don't know what Charlotte likes to read. *The Emigrants* by W.G. Sebald? Perhaps *Play It As It Lays* by Joan Didion might console her. I do know Charlotte chews herself up a lot. *You're an elitist bitch, a fucking snob, get it together you stuck-up clit*, she says to her reflection in the mirror. Sometimes we feel the need to destroy precious things.

What's Wrong With Me

SOMETIMES MY THOUGHTS BECOME SO TANGLED TOGETHER I cannot see where one ends and another begins or I cannot complete a thought as another thought abruptly appears, eventually subsumed by another, so I'm not actually working through a single line of thought towards discovery or mystery (or discovery of mystery) or even the simple satisfaction of letting a thought run its course. What seems like a bundle of fragmented thoughts are projected on the screen of my consciousness around the same time, and it does not seem as if any of these thoughts even originate from me, as if they are passing through me towards other places and never in any kind of orderly fashion. This adds to my confusion over how I know me versus how others, say my wife, colleagues, friends, parents, know me. They do not know this hyper-ruminative me, the me who feels as if he were walking through a thought-thicket of crowded thoughts, slowly untangling spindly thought-branches (laden with thought-prickers) to find my thought-footing. It is *easier* to know myself around people who do not know me. Their not-knowing seems to free me up from my perceived expectations they might have of me. I know myself more easily because I know less of me through their eyes. Whereas my wife knows me at my worst, knows the contradictions in my personality, my common and uncommon behaviors, my propensities, fears, ticks, postures, sources, manifestations of denial, all of it. My sense of her knowledge subsumes my own sense of self. She knows I'm allergic to carrots and cantaloupe and she knows I prefer reading books to speaking to other human beings and she knows I cannot be trusted with a credit card and she knows even what I often do not know, that despite my loneliness and my false (but actual!) sense I am alone in the world, I reach out for her and I reach out for our son and our dogs, she knows this about me!, and she knows other things about me I can't even articulate and of course there are the less intimate ways I feel known by mom and dad and stepmom, all of them different from one another and from the very narrowly defined ways my students know me, very different from my son (who knows what he knows) and the woman at the café walking by my table looking at me as if she wants me to see her seeing me and I want her to see me seeing her being seen and then she's gone and in that moment of her absence, which is inevitable and sudden, death looms. Death is there. The death of subsumed thought, of thoughts incomplete, the death of the body of thought. Sweep up shards of glass glistening in the sun away from which the earth turns. Do you have that in vinyl? I do not know who I am any more than I can see my actual face. I cannot see anything meaningful in what I do or say. I cannot figure out how others perceive me. I cannot see inside their minds to their thoughts. I cannot see what you're thinking. Why isn't somebody knocking on the door right now to take me away from here? To where? To the place that houses people who cannot seem to do anything but hurt himself and others. That thought is somewhat of a lie. I know that. I know I help people. I realize I'm a good father, a half-decent friend and son too. I'm a shitty husband, that is the truth. My thoughts seem to say, *You are alone in everything you do*. Which is to say, I do not think, She's with me, or: He loves me, or: They believe in me. I do think, You are a freak. You can't deal with difficulty and everybody else can. You are alone in wanting to lick a strange woman's pussy. You are alone in Portland. You will never know the name of the tree whose bark is lime green. What am I to do with all of this unused desire? That's another thought that seems

formed by this picture I have of myself as alone in the world. Why
not think, *I need to use up some of thi s desire I have! Let's fuck
today! Today is the day of fucking! Tomorrow is the day of fucking!* I
love seeing a woman's chest uptick or side-slide. I love the shape
of a woman's breasts rising inside her autumn sweater. I love
seeing her tawny fingers (or freckled fingers or long, bony fingers)
curling around a cup of black coffee. Dark hair bangs over pale
skin. O pink lips peach lips thick lips squiggly lips uneven lips!
O buttocks inside black tights! My eyes seek you! My eyes see
yours. Your dark eyes, your green eyes, your blue-gray eyes. What
am I to do with my eyes?! My eyes cannot stop gazing upon the
bodies of strange women! My eyes see only bodies my body wants
to touch but does not. Here I am (alone) at the Grand Canyon.
Here I am (alone) at a diner in Barstow. In this photo I am (alone)
walking the dog. Here I am (alone) with my wife. Here I am
(alone) with God who does not exist in my heart. I have difficulty
imagining my students having any feelings of admiration for me,
which is part of my confusion, not so much I have no idea what
others think of me but I cannot fathom the idea my students
might actually admire me. When my wife gazes at me with something like admiration or appreciation, I turn my eyes away from
her. My eyes do not see her. Did you see her thigh slip out from
beneath her skirt? I did. I always do. In this photo I stand next to
every woman to whom I've ever masturbated. Here I am hiding
beneath the bed so mom and dad cannot find me. Why always in
that order: mom and dad? Why not dad and mom? —Stomp the
snow off your boots, mom says. A student of mine asked me if knew
I was awesome and I thought, no, I do not know I am awesome.
—It's not snow, it's cement, I say. I do know I am sick, sick in my
thoughts, sick in my head, my eyes, my body. My thoughts–and
here they are at their worse–balloon into debilitating worries that
lie, that is to say, they do not speak to me with accuracy about
past, present, or future moments. *You are going to lose your job.
It's out of pity they don't tell you how bad you are. You're a flimsy self-
bitch.* Catastrophic is how my shrink describes them. What feels

painful about catastrophia (made that up) is not so much *thought content* but the frequency and fluency of thought, the textural motion (barbed-like?) of incessant self-interruption, water flooding the hull, a deck of cards with edges like shards flung inside a cockpit, an expulsion of pet dander, an endless list of every person I have disappointed or hurt and will disappoint or hurt combined with an endless list of all of the problems I have caused for myself. My damaged marriage, my uncontrollable impulses, my impossible desire, my unparagraphed prose. My face suddenly feels hot and wet, as if everything were collapsing inside me, crumbling against the backside of my face, as if the backside of my face were an inverted bowl filling up with the warm effluvia of sorrow. My thoughts become self-pitying, self-obliterating. William Styron (somebody must have called him Bill) writes in *Darkness Visible: A Memoir of Madness*:

> Of the many dreadful manifestations of the disease, both physical and psychological, a sense of self-hatred–or, put less categorically, a failure of self-esteem–is one of the most universally experienced symptoms, and I had suffered more and more from a general feeling of worthlessness as the malady had progressed.

Mudhoney sings, *When tomorrow hits / it will hit you hard*. This *sense* of self-hatred (as Styron says) is expressed via self talking to self, thoughts of paranoia, of self-consciousness, or self-reflexive thoughts, clearly irrational and unfounded. Lies. Self lies to self. Here's a photo of me with my self-disgust (I'm the one swinging the baton). Oddly enough my thoughts of self-loathing are more fully formed but strafe-like and extended, an all-night rave of doom. I haven't seen you in forever, I owe like ten people emails, I'm worried you didn't like me, I think I came off a little too stern, I didn't even know I was scowling or grimacing or smiling, I cannot register till I pay off what I cannot pay off, there's a warrant out for my car, out for my arrest, the fraud police are on their way. My self-loathing is like a school of piranha (as in the 1978 movie *Piranha*), tiny flesh-eating fish tearing through skin, rending vessels, ligaments, muscle, and bone, turning me into nothing. Here's a photo of me on a runway at the bottom of the ocean floor. There does not seem an end to thought, or perhaps the end of thought is death. My writing this very sentence does console me, I mean, I feel the pleasure of expressing my thoughts, of assembling words and phrases into sentences and knowing those sentences are miniature self-portraits showing something aside from self-hatred, the self who makes things, who tries to make things, the self speaking to self, who tries to be a good person, I, the person writing this, creating a representation of voice that is not me but *of me*. I'm kind to others, I cheer for others, I love my son, I express my love for my son to my son, I try harder to love my wife. These thoughts, these conversations (via prose) between self and self, are what? The imaginative trying to lift itself out of the barbed ruminative? A symptom of mental illness? As much as I want my thoughts to slow down and become less fragmented–I do–what would I do without them? Who would I be If I didn't have a crowded consciousness? One of those cyclists who wear those terrible Spandex shorts? Cyclists of America, your shorts terrify me! Can you hear the lovely static of self whispering to self? I can hear the static of self whispering to self. My wife asked me today why I always return to this place of hopelessness and doom, why can't I stop thinking of things as irreparably broken, why can't I see that I'm not alone in the world? A person is not an illness, a person becomes ill, a person gets better, I am not getting better. Tony says, *We are amazed how hurt we are. / We would give anything for what we have.* Pavement says, *Because there's 40 different shades of black*. Self says, *When tomorrow hits it hits hard.*

On Talking With Carlos

I GET EASILY DISTRACTED WITH TALK ABOUT THE WEATHER or weekend plans or the new restaurants in the neighborhood or how many days till the weekend arrives. I prefer a more rigorous discussion that takes talkers through a variety of mindstates and emotions, a conversation that toggles between dissemblance and confession, silliness and sobriety. Talk devoid of small talk. Today's outlook is partly fucked up. I like to rant, to mock. I don't mind getting caustic over somebody else's ignorance. Otherwise silence is just fine with me. My masseuse and friend Carlos loves serious, responsive conversations—idea speak, he calls it. He likes to mix anecdote and reportage with philosophical inquiry. He digresses, he interrupts, he scoffs. He never conceals his feelings, may it be confusion or truculence or despair. No topic is too dark, too explicit, or too grotesque for Carlos. Rubbing my shoulder or thumb-kneading my neck, Carlos expounds on some of Kierkegaard's ideas on anxiety or describes a scene from his favorite novel, Knut Hamsun's *Hunger* or tells me his worst fear about death (that his brother would spit on his casket, upsetting any grandchildren present—children, Carlos believes, should attend funerals) or the way his father liked to walk around the house (even eat breakfast) wearing only a jock-strap. Carlos describes his father's penis as *thick like a stretched-out Slinky*. There's no tiptoeing around sex with this guy. You run into him on the street and he tells you about his wife not letting him *put it in her behind*. Carlos is German. He thinks Americans suffer from

Cheerful Mania. When you ask people how they are in America, they're great. Everything's just wonderful. Holidays and vacations are described as *amazing* or *a blast* even though they fought the entire drive to Taos or got intestinal worms from an over-priced restaurant in Sedona or grandpa swatted one of the grand-kids and said in his defense, *I hit you plenty of times and look at how you turned out*. Nobody even waters down bad news like they did when I was a kid (e.g., He's down to a half-pack a day!). We've stopped telling others bad news. We're afraid to tell the truth. Carlos says Europeans don't chitchat. Two horrific world wars plus communism stomped that out. Chitchat is denial, and the source of any denial state is death. Carlos insists I imagine my death routinely in order to stay healthy. I ask him what he thinks the least painful death might be. He tells me a bullet wound to the parietal lobe switches the lights right off. I tell Carlos I'm not the kind of person who owns a gun or touches other people's guns and he kneels just beneath the face rest so I can see his squinty smirk. —You're the kind of person who smokes the toke, Carlos says. He calls me a *sissynik* and returns to stretching out my calves. If you want to see Carlos get really pissy, ask him how he's doing and then walk away before he can answer. He says Americans do this all the time. He calls such a person, depending on gender, *Hussy-Woman* or Mr. Fecal-Face. Carlos says he's heartbroken because people eat animals and animals have souls. I ask Carlos about the people who must fill a beautiful silence with inane, uplifting banter. In the elevator or break room or wait-ing area at the DMV or on an airplane or around a play structure in the neighborhood park: everywhere it seems folks cannot stop speaking about topics that mean very little to them. Talking about unimportant matters is very easy to do. Also easy is talking about something about which you know very little. Admittedly Carlos does this all the time. He believes the former President Bush napped two hours a day; swears that his sister-in-law doesn't wear underpants (his word: *underpanties*). Carlos believes a silence is the entrance one takes to one's mind: beautiful and

ugly thoughts, obsessions, night haunts, fantasies of pussy, of cock.
—No, Carlos tells me, —People don't want to listen to their
thoughts. Thinking means ripping off the scab and letting blood
stain the skin. Means looking down into that hole and seeing a
dead body. One dead body is every dead body. Means no solutions.
Means you put up and put up and put up. Means fraga. Means
you'll never give birth to a baby of your own. Means your wish is
granted. —There is only silence in conversation, Carlos tells me.
I ask Carlos how he deals with these chatter bitches. And he drops
my leg to the table and lowers his mouth to my ear, so close I hear
the moist parting of his lips.

Man in the Bubble

I DON'T ENJOY PICNICS. THEY OFFER ME NO PLEASURE, just misery, well maybe that's overstating it, not misery but irritation or better put, mild suffering. First, it's plain impossible to find a flat stretch of grass on which to spread your blanket. Last I checked the earth was round. Any slight shift or spasm and drinks and condiments tip over, spilling sticky liquids or sauces on the blanket or a leg or hand. When picnicking I try to keep still. I tense the muscles in my legs and arms and shoulders as if I were pretending to be a statue but how relaxing is that? In order to drink, eat, pass condiments, play the harmonica, sneeze, you must move your body, which in turn threatens to dismantle all picnic order. I don't mean to sound whiny but it's a lot of work to stand up from sitting on the ground in a crouched position. Unpretzeling my leg out from under my ass I knock over a bottle of wine or jar of pickles. What if I have an itch I must scratch? There go the black olives. And why am I suddenly standing up? Perhaps I've forgotten something in the car or, worst-case scenario (my largest source of anxiety, no that's not true, I take that back), a fly or mosquito or bee or wasp hovers over the potato salad or salami slices. I can't enjoy conversation and tony finger foods if a legion of ants are headed for my ankle, or even if no insects threaten my person, because of my high anxiety surrounding picnics I *feel* ants crawling all over my body. Mosquitoes buzz my ear even when my ear and the area around my ear is totally clear. I don't know how horses do it. I admit, I enjoy the convenience my 800 square feet of house offer. You have to go to the bathroom? Wash your hands with soap? Need a shower? Are you sleepy? Would you like to read your favorite novel in the comfort of a made bed? Eating at the dinner table in my kitchen, I'm like five seconds from the next activity. At a picnic's end there are messes to clean and stuff to pack and a blanket to shake out and fold up. Wipe the dirt off your behind. I hate dirty feet. Walk back to the car, drive home. And once home, unpack the car. I don't know about you but I like to keep my chores to a minimum. What's easier than sitting in a chair or lying in bed? Inside or outside I usually stay away from jams, fruit, candy, or chocolate. I don't like my hands or chin or lips to get all sticky. Admit it. It's a struggle to wipe hands clean while holding onto a drink or balancing a plate on one's lap so it doesn't tip over. If you want me to go on a picnic, supply me with extra hands, like five or six, to handle all picnicking logistics. Can you pass me the horseradish, please? The drinking straws are underneath the bottle opener. What should I do with the bones and the seeds and the pits? Oh no, the napkin blew away! If it is a windy day, one must take additional time to design and build (then execute, which means making adjustments too) a defense system in which weighted objects pin to the ground paper plates (or paper lined in wicker) and cloth and/or paper napkins and assorted wrappers and baggies. This is a lot of work. Meanwhile flies and ants and sweat bees begin to swarm. To picnic one needs an army of soldiers, engineers, and builders. I guess I'm not really ordering my reasons here – this is a discussion we're having, right? – but let's just say this next one is a biggie. Allergies. Any extended time (20 minutes plus) spent outside during spring or summer, the months when everybody plans picnics, can trigger a sneeze attack lasting anywhere from a second to six hours. These sneezes are immense, like a buffalo in a restroom stall. They shake the furniture. I swear to God – and I know a doctor might disagree with me on this one – when I sneeze, my brain shimmies forward in my skull. If one of these skull sneezes overtakes me at a picnic any piece of food I'm holding might end up on my lap or worse on somebody else's. Imagine eating a Triscuit spread with spicy artichoke heart dip and snot glob. Did I mention I have food allergies? Carrots, watermelon, cantaloupe, apples, blond cherries – all the picnic staples. If I were to eat any of these foods my throat would swell and get itchy and to scratch such an itch I rub my throat with the tip of my tongue, which makes this clicking clatter. As a child that sound akin to skin scraping asphalt irritated my older brother so much he'd punch me in the arm and I'm afraid it doesn't end there.

So Hard It Bleeds

SAY I DREAM OF MIRANDA JULY, A CONVERSATION REGARD-
ing Pretend in Film or an interview about her fiction or a kiss we
share, my fingers tugging her underpants over her hipbone, and
right then some part of the actual Miranda July hurts. That's
right, my fantasy of her causes *her* pain – not a debilitating pain
but a squeeze in a joint or a pulsating ache in the temple or
the foot. I don't know Miranda July and I mean Miranda July no
harm, for I admire her work and intend to read and/or witness
her art as long as she makes it and as long as I continue to live.
In my little what if, I'm not aware my fantasies or thoughts of
Miranda July result in her feeling ill and it doesn't matter what
Miranda July's doing or where Miranda July is: eating a burrito
in Los Angeles, yoga in Amsterdam, daydreaming in Reykjavik
(thus inadvertently hurting somebody else), driving through
Gresham on her way to Mount Hood. Whatever. Her blood loses
oxygen, her blood pressure raises, no, she becomes dehydrated
and scuttles to the kitchen for a glass of water (on the phone
with her parents Miranda July says she finds herself drinking so
much water lately, like 15 to 20 glasses per day; —What size are
the glasses you drink from? Her father asks, —Are we talking
about a pint glass?) or maybe her feet blister or she's struck by
spells of nausea or develops new allergies to carrots, bananas, soy,
has to nap more during the day to make up for lost sleep at night
and yes, her work falters. Instead of making four award-winning
films and writing three novels (one nominated for an NBA) in 20

years Miranda July barely finishes one unfocused film and no
book or no, one book widely panned and another book nobody
reviews, even bloggers stay away from it, all because I cannot
curb my fantasies of Miranda July, which now happen frequently
and become for me a heightened source of anxiety. The fantasies
are more sexual, feeling-filled, as in me flicking her taut breasts
or the two of us holding each other on a street corner after a
horrible day, our embrace shielding us from the heavy traffic of
cars and bicycles and pedestrians, the day's mayhem of voice
mails and self-imposed pressure to make something goddamn
better held at bay like a song on pause, her fingers tickling the
back of my neck, mine lightly scratching the inside of her arm.
Touch lightly the skin over your eyelids or the bridge of your nose
and you feel relief. With each new dream, the real Miranda July
hurts, e.g., paper cuts, nicotine cravings, heart burn, fouled
spark plugs and as years pass I peruse magazines for a Miranda-
July interview that might reveal information about the next
Miranda-July project but come up empty handed. I can't even find
a Miranda-July short story in a small press literary magazine
and more years pass and her work disappears because she spends
so much time dealing with her arthritic hands and her addiction
to Percocet and headaches so painful she must endure them in a
dark, quiet room. Panic attacks, frantic Mondays, days of low-
to high-grade depression. Even though Miranda July chooses to
dress and feed and clean herself and make the day's appointments, none of it chips away at the loneliness she feels or at her
gurgling anxiety that is like pacing back and forth in a window-
less, white-walled conference room, hard stepping it wall to wall,
not at all seeing the open door that leads to open air, only that
elfin-like inner prowler knocking about the skull. Some days she
slides back the curtain and mistakes early morning for a new
day. An easy, tedious chore like transferring wet, heavy clothes
from washer to dryer is enough to make her go irrevocably mad.
The point of no reality. Doctors, naturopaths, Chinese doctors,
therapists, life coaches, palm readers – nobody can figure out the

origins of Miranda July's symptoms, nobody can realize my obsessive daydreaming besets her with suffering so nobody tells me to stop, tells me what I'm doing is hurtful, a soul killer I am, nobody shakes me and says, —Get out of your head. Play Scrabble or call your mom or knit a sweater, give your dogs a bath. Anything. Stop hurting this hugely talented and young artist-writer-filmmaker with your secret thoughts of her! The drafting of this story alone causes Miranda July at a dinner party with friends in Koreatown to bite her lip so hard it bleeds.

The Manuscript (III)

OUR SEX LIFE BECAME STRAINED. IT'S NOT THAT I'D HURT my wife, it's that I *continued* to hurt my wife and to give her credit where credit is mostly due, my wife tried her hardest to forgive me, but how could she forgive me if I was not even finished hurting her? My wife would get into bed and say to me, —I think you're cute, and I'd smile at her without setting aside the book I was reading or if she really wanted sex or thought we should have sex, that is, thought it beneficial to our marriage or that I needed the physical release, she asked, —How about some sex? And about half the time, that is half the time I did not feel like fucking my wife, I relented. I mean to say, I felt ashamed we were failing at marriage, so fucking would somehow indicate otherwise? When I wanted sex, I'd set aside my book, snap the light off, and say, —We could have sex, which, in its use of the hypothetical modal *could*, expresses latent dissatisfaction, as if I were saying, we could have sex but instead we sit in bed and read our books or sleep and either activity – sex or no sex – is a suitable way to pass the time. So now I tried to be more direct, more honest in expressing my desire. I'd say, —I want to have sex with you. Or: —Do you want to have sex with me? Neither of us used the phrase *make love.* During intercourse we would use the word *fuck*, as in, —Fuck me, or —I like to fuck you. We had intercourse about once a week or once every two weeks if one of us was actually not feeling well or if I or my wife were feeling despondent about our marriage, lonely inside of it, which happened frequently. We did not often have sex more than once a week, the exception when one of us had been away or one of us was feeling, as they say, extra horny, a word neither of us, especially my wife, really liked to say, and if we did, we said it in a quieter voice and only in bed. Our sex seemed fairly routine although I didn't know what other marrieds' sex lives were like to know what was and was not routine because nobody ever talked about it. Novels and short stories might enact or dramatize marital conflict but rarely (if ever) do they talk about it. I'm talking about it. Our sex seemed fairly routine. We didn't play role games or wear costumes or use sex toys or talk dirty or masturbate in front of each other. I didn't slap my wife's buttocks, and she didn't moan and scream as if she were giving birth. We were shy with each other and we didn't try to move beyond our shyness. (So very Midwestern we were.) We'd kiss and touch each other's bodies and then our hands would begin to rub each other's genitals. I'd reach for my wife's much faster than she'd reach for mine. If I touched her too soon, my wife would flinch, as if her head or her body (or both) did not want my touch, but could be slowly persuaded only if I touched her gently. *Non-sexual* or *sensual* touch, she called it. She said if I would touch her throughout the day in this more sensual way, her body would be more ready to receive sexual touch. All of this seemed so complicated to me, like what she really needed was this time for her mind to let go of its hurt, anger, and loneliness, to *fall* into an illusion of intimacy that would allow her body to withstand (dare I say, enjoy?) my touch. We rarely asked each other to try a new position or technique. We did not consult the *Kama Sutra*. We did not view pornography. Smoking weed worked for us like an aphrodisiac, increasing our desire and the urgency to touch each other sexually. Stoned, she was more likely to touch my genitals and let me touch hers soon after we began, or she might let me go down on her, which I loved to do but she didn't seem to enjoy it because she'd pull me off her after a minute or two. Perhaps my cunnilingus techniques were misguided and crude. I'd move my tongue as if I were a dog lapping up water after a long walk on a humid day and she'd say, —Slow down, or —Not so hard. At some point, she had stopped fellating me, but why should she? I never let her finish me off because I wanted to fuck her. One of David Foster Wallace's narrators talks about how selfish it is for a man to not let his partner have the pleasure of taking her man to orgasm, and I guess I see his narrator's point. Without exception I used my finger to make my wife come, and then we fucked. If my wife and I were very stoned, our sex felt urgent, was somewhat athletic (not to be confused with acrobatic). I liked to see the front of my wife's body, below mine or atop, straddled. We'd come pretty hard, never at the same time. The whole thing lasted about 20 minutes, at the most, and then we'd say our I-love-yous and hug for ten seconds tops and then she'd go to the bathroom and I'd amble to the kitchen for a glass of water. If we smoked weed, we might have sex outside of the bedroom, usually in front of the TV or in my office on the pullout couch, and on occasion, maybe once a year, we had sex in the car or in a public restroom at a restaurant, but it had been like five years since we'd done that. My wife preferred lying down to standing up, preferred the bed to the couch or the floor (or a table or toilet seat or against the wall) whereas I preferred any place but the bedroom, in bed. The sex in my dreams happened in closed-in work or service spaces, e.g., a bathroom, stairwell, janitor's closet, a kitchenette in a motor home. Sex in bed was too plausible, too ordinary, not impossible enough, as if I wanted the fucking to zap any semblance of domestic functionality. When we stayed in a hotel or a motel we had sex. No explanation needed. My wife did not wear lingerie, and I didn't wear silk pajamas, and we preferred it that way. I wished she wore only her panties (to her I say, *underpants*) and a tank top that fit closely over her chest, but she often wore, out of desire for comfort, roomy, tattered flannel pajama bottoms and an oversized T-shirt. Admittedly I wanted to be comfortable too, so I wore only underwear to bed, but she wished I'd wear long underwear or silk pajama bottoms. She especially liked me to wear my long underwear bottoms but rarely did I wear them – and not because they bothered me but because I'd grown into the habit of not pleasing her. I thought of what I wanted, what pleased me or made me comfortable before I considered what she might want, what might be nice for me to give to her. We tended to recoil at each other's desire. My penis size seemed average, maybe smaller than average. As I got older, I masturbated less. I assumed my wife masturbated but was not sure when or where. I liked smelling her. Even though it seemed like a trend for women to shave their montes pubis, I nursed a three-decade long pubic-hair fetish, so my wife's large tuft of black pubic hair attracted me (still does) although if she did want to shave it off, I would want (out of curiosity or something deeper than that, whatever makes men desire the illusion of virginity) to touch that new smooth skin and the even smoother inside her. This reminds me of the way some women like to feel a bald man's head. Once or twice I gave her a pointer on handjobs (funny word) but she didn't always remember; just as I forgot she preferred me to rub with my fore-finger, slowly and lightly, as if I were handling a contact lens and not a tooth brush. She liked a soft, slight touch and I liked a hard, fast touch. The word *panties* sounded pornographic to her, like it instantly conjured up intercourse between untoward strangers or that which stood in the way of their untoward intercourse. When she heard the word panties, did she also hear the word *panting*? Or *phantom*? Or did she also hear the phrase *fuck me*? I'm not a fan of the word *cock*. The tone of that word – throaty and ribald – is off-putting to me. We were not generous with our desire for each other. Perhaps we felt we didn't have much to extend, or we feared what would happen if we did lavish each other with our desire, or perhaps we simply didn't know how to offer our-selves to each other with generous abandon, that is, for whatever reason, for better or worse, in our lives we had had very little practice. We were not very good lovers for each other. Even though we could improve, we chose not to. How many couples experi-enced the difficulty of trying to be closer to each other, and better to each other? How many people experienced the difficulty of satisfying their own desires while attempting to help their spouse or partner satisfy their desires? I didn't know if other couples experienced this difficulty. I assumed they did. I had to assume if I experienced it, others did, but I didn't know for sure because nobody seemed to talk about it. Let's start talking about it. So maybe we can feel less alone in the world. I preferred sex in the morning, my wife preferred sex at bedtime. I didn't always wear underpants. I faked headaches. My wife seemed to know I was not there for her and I knew she knew this, yet neither of us were willing to speak aloud. We were most pleased with each other when we were fucking very, very hard, at least it seemed that way to me. This hard fucking (silly phrase) seemed to emanate and express our mutual anger, her pissed off at me for rejecting her again and again and me angry because she was not a figment but an actual woman whom I didn't know how to relate to or how to touch, my dear, pissed-off wife pulling me into her harder and saying, —Fuck me harder and me pummeling her harder and faster as if we could fully express our anger. Writing that gives me a little hard-on.

BOOBS AND WET pubes, buttocks and ample breasts, red pubic hair beneath sheer panties, parted slit and pink labia, dear Jehovah, lightly daub clitoris while finger-swiping the areola of Allah, flick nipple too but when pussy excretion mixes with saliva or a pubic hair clasps tongue of the Lord our Son, trace the lower rise of breast, heft its suck, mouth the nipple straw-like, Buddha Buddha, making circular motions with tongue-tip around the nub of clitoris and into the vagina we go, hipbone bumping buttocks, circling finger around the anus, insert, then raise legs in the air like banners of the Christ Our Lord wind-blown, fuck-holler, fuck-breathe, nose-squeal, flood her standing up, Yahweh, the standing power fuck a.k.a. the S P F, tight ringlets of curly brown pubic hair the shape of Mother Mary. God Bless the Holy Pussy.

MY FRIENDSHIPS WITH women were often founded, then cultivated, in mutual despair. It was like a door through which together we walked. One held it open for the other or we stepped across the threshold at the same time and the door frame for a brief instant contained us. Sharing with each other the awful mess of our lives seemed to strengthen our friendship. It buoyed the illusion that only we could save each other. Rarely did we talk about anything good or uplifting. To do that was to acknowledge we could not save each other (or we didn't want to be saved) and our friendship was narrowly focused. We only presented to each other a single part of our personalities, which we liked to believe was oneiric and ubiquitous. By deeply exploring those parts with each other, we seemed to move within reach of each other. We inquired, moved in and out of awareness, trafficked in *real feeling*, postured. We consoled, we stood in. It was as if we were cleaning and dressing each other's wounds. Soothing each other. Frannie and I would email each other four, five times per week, discussing past depressive episodes, her off-again-off-again boyfriend, literature. Awaiting replies I'd check my email about ten times per day. More like ten times in 90 minutes. Between sending and receiving a reply, I'd reread the message I had typed. And again. *Dear Frannie* was a word-hug. *I really enjoyed talking with you over coffee* meant can we have coffee always. The word *really* said next time let's scoot into a quiet nook and hold hands. To her, the whole message likely expressed my lonely man's desperation. I took more pleasure in reading my emails to her, for it was the dream of woman not an actual woman that aroused in me mellifluous feeling. Opening a message I'd typed to Frannie I could imagine her at a café or a laundromat, laptop on lap, tip of tongue arcing over her upper lip as she turned over my words, held them up to afternoon's jittery light to punch out their pointed meanings. I'd imagine her feeling desired, chased after in this secretive way. Perhaps my electronic gaze annoyed her. Perhaps married men tired her and she deleted the emails. If Frannie didn't send a reply, again I'd read back over

the original message I'd sent to see if anything I'd written might
have offended her or expressed my feelings in a way too obvious
or direct instead of ambiguous or coded. I believed I could toe
the line between desiring her outright and admiring her safely
from a platonic distance. Presently I don't believe I'm capable
of having a purely *platonic relations*hip with a woman, that is to
say, I think it impossible to have a close friendship *free* of desire.
Perhaps I keep my close friendships with women in order to not
only stir my desire but to construct psychic storage spaces in
which my desire can dwell. I mean, we *were* friends and Frannie
knew me in the way I wanted to be known (sad, broken)
and because I was older (I know, smacks of cliché, older man and
younger woman) I had a few wise things to say about being
in your 20s she found helpful. She was self-involved and broken-
hearted and I couldn't help but want to coddle-fuck her. She told
me her boyfriend was the love of her life but treated her poorly
sometimes (not all the time) and did too much blow despite the
fact Frannie was a recovering addict. I'd met her boyfriend,
and he was a decent guy, a guy with whom I could imagine as a
friend. Tragic and unstable, yes, young, yes. He had the mindset
I'd had in my 20s, that you always felt your life had not yet begun.
It started once you finished grad school or law school or medical
school or became published or checked in and out of and back
in rehab or earned that promotion or married then birthed a child
but really this was a mindset of avoidance. Life had begun. Life
was happening. Life is my son napping as my wife stacks warm
plates atop the dishwasher. Life is me in a room typing the word,
word. I mean, didn't we all snuff out the present moment for
dreams of the next thing or memories of the past? Men especially
seemed to suffer unnecessarily from a sense of entitlement as
if eminent stardom awaited but nobody ever discovered us men
and I told Frannie that. My wife assumed I was at work but here I
was sitting across from Frannie at a café, nibbling on a cookie she'd
bought for me. Frannie was an intelligent woman but young too,
not used to a man talking in such a thoughtful, honest way about

desperate-male states. I could feel myself performing for her, like a show-off, a star acting not so much out of sincerity but out of desire and self-consciousness, as if I were framing a picture of me for me. My body pitched towards her lap as her fingertip nagged at a nick in the table's surface not two inches from my right hand. I believe a man can love two women. Falling in love with non-wife woman does not necessarily cancel out or even diminish love for wife. I believe this. Many years ago, just after my wife and I married, I wrote a story (title: "Here's to You, Mrs. Robinson") about a man named Henry, an anesthetist. Henry initiates a dalliance with a college-aged woman named Clarissa who shares with Henry everything his wife cannot. A destructive, cynical soul. Punk-era effrontery. Obsession with her favorite film *The Graduate*. Transient atmospherics (e.g., thickly glazed donuts, americanos, magic mushrooms). Glossy black lipstick and tight, kinky curls. Sexual Wooowwwww. Yet Henry loves his wife (name I cannot recall), for she's *mother*, the immovable center of their family and even though his wife has become, in the decade past, materialistic and career-prone and bored by Henry's academic pursuits, Henry cannot leave his family. Crow mates with crow unto death. Henry takes strange pleasure in the silence draped over the unused furniture of their marriage. Imagine a ride in the Range Rover to some indolent dinner party in the hills. They don't attempt conversation, peremptory or otherwise, instead the emptiness of their lives traps them in an instance in which neither her Dolce & Gabbana sprees nor his coed mistress can save them from this helpless hole called existence and his feelings swell for his wife and their history together, memories of their boys, their boys' futures, the city of Berkeley—all of this binds them and like it or not, it's his wife, not Clarissa, who attends his death bed (45 years later) yet the last thought that passes through Henry's consciousness is a memory of Clarissa standing on her toes tipped to reach a glass pitcher atop the refrigerator in her apartment. Both women scald his soul. That is a story I created from my imagination governed by desire and loneliness.

Of course the love Henry feels for his wife is different than the love Henry feels for his mistress. One is a love of endurance and accumulation, the love of comfort, of familiar skin creases below the cheeks or around mouth corners or a wallet or a buckeye one keeps without reason. The other love is a clean slice through flesh. A quiver. One is water, the other blood. Romantic? Yes, though it's a decent attempt at story (I don't much like it now, don't like the way I hide behind the *Anesthetist* mask) and it predates this writing, although when I wrote that story, I had feelings for poetess Frannie, and I admit my love for barista Frannie or the dream of my love for barista Frannie, along with time spent with Frannie, did in fact diminish my wife to lowly roommate status. We shared a house, a mortgage, a couple dogs, and now we had a child. So yes, I believe a man can love more than one woman but that wasn't exactly the case for me. It was what I told myself to deny the fact I'd stopped loving my wife and to justify my attraction to a woman not my wife. Frannie, as I said, was a reader of Russian literature and in my mind I compared her to Julie Christie's *Lara*, sad, beautiful Lara, from the film adaptation of Pasternak's *Doctor Zhivago*, which happened to be mine and my wife's favorite movie. If Frannie were Lara, then I was Zhivago, a generous man, poet, passionate reader of literature (although I don't recall seeing Omar Sharif's character toting around a book much less reading one), a man who loves his wife in the way one loves the mother of his child: with awe and respect, with an intense sibling-like affection (Zhivago and Tonia are cousins, actually) that's protective and lacks intimacy but not devotion; Zhivago loves his mistress Lara in the way one loves a soulmate. (Oh, how I despise that Hallmark phrase, *soulmate* – especially the way it glistens with the illusion of eternity, of forever, as if we are not *in decay*, as if we are not divided within.) A desperately obsessive love, one he can never fully express. Zhivago tries to stay faithful to Tonia but cannot. I began to imagine my relationship with Frannie in a such a light – that is, I was trying to stay faithful to my wife while still maintaining these secret feelings for Frannie but unbeknownst to me, *the au-thor*, infidelity lay ahead like an ecstatic ocean into which I would sink and float and splash about all at once. I didn't love my wife as Zhivago loves Tonia. It seemed any affection I once had for my wife disappeared. This Zhivago comparison removed me further from the more central problem I no longer felt any love (or wished to feel love) for my wife. At home I became distracted. Frannie (and whatever color bra she'd been wearing the previous afternoon) would appear in masturbation fantasies. At the dinner table my wife prattled on about her day at work while in my mind Frannie and I strolled Cal's campus at dusk. Yellow streetlights dotted the Berkeley hills and we talked about books or movies or about some depraved story in the news, children in Iraq dying in some chemical blast, a sexual predator back on the streets, the kind of talk my wife and I could never have because she withstood enough human depravity at her job. —Are you listening to me? My wife asked. —Of course. Go on. —About what? —You know. —I know I know, but you obviously don't, my wife said, mashing her thumb into her white bread. After dinner I'd check my email. At some point Frannie mentioned she liked *tiny* objects so I began passing her *tiny* notes on which I'd write critical thoughts about a book she was reading. I wanted to impress her with my *humble* intelligence. At work I'd print out these notes, trim the paper into a thin strip the size of a pocket watch, fold and write her name on back, and then at the café, slide it to her with my debit card. Frannie was an intuitive woman. Surely she could feel my desire for her tumbling out of those tiny scraps of paper yet nothing was ever spoken between us and because I couldn't read her mind, I never knew how she felt about me but I could surmise (my shrink has my back on this) she understood how strong my feelings for her were. Last night I dreamt dad presents me with a plaque on which is engraved my name next to the words *Divorce, Granted by the State of Illinois* (where dad now lives with his second wife) and I feel relief my

marriage is finally over followed by an appreciation for dad
because who better than him understands what my heart needs.

I DIDN'T WANT my wife to think I was capable of disappointing
her or hurting others. (Of course I was.) That's one of my struggles. I don't like to disappoint others. I do anything to keep from
disappointing somebody else. At a restaurant if my food is
tepid or just plain bad I refuse to send it back for fear I'm inconve-
niencing the waitress or waiter, then cook. And what if the server
or cook is already having a difficult day? My demand might
cause them to lash out at me or another person. They might be
upset with me. At work I hate to request from my boss days off
or ask for a raise. Whether I deserve days off or the pay increase
pales to the notion such a request means my boss might scruti-
nize her feelings about me. I don't like the idea I have an effect on
others. I secret away any conflicting and potentially hurtful feelings as if out in the world, outside of my consciousness, those
feelings can only cause pain to others and I cannot cause pain to
others. (Of course I can.) Seeing another person suffering
because of something I said or did forces me to confront the core
of what I believe about myself, that I'm not a good person, that I
don't want to change. And it is not simply a matter of me avoiding
conflict: it is this old feeling I perpetrate all wrongdoings and
ransack all souls or at the least I irritate everybody around me.
Every song is about me. As a child my older brothers told me the
floor of the backseat was the most comfortable place to ride
and they let me have it all to myself. I never understood my wife's
inclination to surround herself with others: ladies' salon, theme
parties, dinner parties. I was a recluse. Still am. Morbid too.
Meek. Don't forget socially awkward. Know I know I run myself
down. I get that. I know the self I present is different from the
person my friends and family perceive me to be. The weather is
largely inside of me and tomorrow's forecast calls for more stifle
and arrest. Walk in the walk-in closet to find it emptied. Sometimes the only thing to do is undo. I told my wife I had feelings for

Frannie but they were so private (thought I) and detached from reality, it would be unfair for my wife to see Frannie as *the other woman*. —Fantasy is medication, I said. —A soothing habit, an escape, I said that (or something like that) to my wife. —OK, my wife said, —So Frannie is innocent. The point is you *want* to escape our marriage. Outside rain water poured from the gutter spout onto the front stoop. A car's headlights swept over my wife's face. Her cheeks were sunken, damp lashes blinked away tears and spittle teetered off her lower lip. Her despair attracted me. In her pain I felt known, closer to her. I wanted to fuck. What I wanted was bad. In bed my wife's despair over my rejection of her drew me to her. My fingertip swabbed her chin and cheek and I told her that I loved her, which I did, sort of, and I didn't want to escape our marriage (a lie, a part of me did). Our sex that night was (no surprise) obstreperous and angry. Post-orgasm (mine), holding my wife in my arms, my mind's eye dreamed up Frannie and me lying on a couch, not mine and my wife's couch, some other couch of brushed suede with pliant cushions. We're holding each other like Hansel and Gretel might have if the witch hadn't imprisoned them in her kitchen with its sweet cider smell and preheating oven of death. I told my wife I'd like our sex to become more lively, unpredictable, experimental even, which in turn might make me feel less lonely, less apt to draw into fantasy. Although to suggest my dreams of Frannie were purely sexual reduced my feelings for her, but I needed to buoy the illusion love was not just a word my wife and I trotted out to conceal its absence. That is to say, in theory, I wanted to play *the husband* character opposite my wife as *the wife* character yet the real-me was another character who not only loved *the other woman* char-acter but squirmed in the character roles of *responsible father* and *house owner* and *community member*. Such roles were for others. Instead I said, —For men sexual touch creates intimacy. I asked, —Can't you dirty-talk me? Just a little. I said, —Our sex bores me. —When you try to get me to talk dirty, my wife said, leaning up in bed, flipping on the lamp, yellow light spraying across her pinched face, my wife said, —When you say things like, *should I fuck you harder*, or whenever you use the words, *pussy, wet pussy, my cock*, or *big cock*, our sex begins to feel artificial and mechanical, as in *Insert Finger Here*, or like a cliché, like some porno, which mutes the feelings I have for you, I mean, why do men want women to act so slutty? And I'm sorry but I'm not interested in anal penetration. You're going to have to live with that one. My anus was not designed for penile penetration and yes, *penile* is a word. —I haven't asked you for butt sex in years. —Last month you did. —The point is I'm OK not having butt sex. —The point is I need you to touch me outside of the bedroom and to not recoil at my touch and to not turn so frigid when I hug you. Those goddamn half-hugs you give. It's like I'm diseased. —I can't help it. That's how I react. It's a gut thing. —So your gut reaction is to not want touch from your wife? And please don't use this conversation in your writing. —Of course not, I said. My wife snapped off the lamp and buried herself under the thick duvet as I lay in the vaulted dark. Against my wife's wishes, I'm using that conversation or my memory of that conversation (memory as dream, memory as tableau of the present moment) and it might seem like a betrayal (OK, it is a betrayal) but not as harmful as the self-deception I have practiced for most of my life. That is, I betray my own wishes for the wishes of others (or what I perceive as the wishes of others) so what I want is secondary to the degree I stop seeing myself and instead see only the self others create for me.

A PHOTOGRAPH FROM our wedding reception: my wife and her grandmother, their faces blushed with drink and touched by fortune and comfort, and behind them, in the photograph's background, I stand by myself, my hands empty and my face expressing anxiety and gall bordering on rage. I look like a lunatic. My eyes seem to throb and my jaw juts as if it were wired shut. I'm guessing the social interaction a wedding reception demands gave rise to this foul mood, not my wedding day, of which I have

fond memories: the ceremony we carefully designed and orches-
trated; the beauty and dignity of my wife; being surrounded by
all these people from all parts of our lives. Yet I don't recall our
wedding photographer shooting this photo nor do I recall standing by myself at my own wedding reception or behind my wife
and her grandmother. This instance feels outside of time and of
my memory of that experience, yet the look on my face speaks
honestly to me now (as I view the photograph many years later)
of my feelings about marriage, more honestly than I speak to my
wife or close friends or extended family. Dread or anger folded
me back inside myself, far away from the jovial festivity of our
wedding reception, shaping my countenance. We cannot see all
of the faces we present. My wife calls her husband in that photo,
Evil Jay. My wife and I laugh not because it's far-fetched but
because the photo and her title, like the punchline of a joke, draw
together two seemingly disparate elements: marriage and malice.
Or perhaps me and malice.

I ADMIT, I talked too much about Frannie to my wife for her
not to think, *Does he have feelings for this barista?* In our kitchen,
opening cans of lentil soup or tomato paste, laying spoon, knife
(blade out), and fork atop cloth napkins, feet slippered and sliding around Marmoleum, I'd speak to my wife about another
woman in carefully affected impartiality, attempting to stifle any
joy rising from my heart yet unbeknownst to me, the frequency
with which Frannie guest-starred in my reports of the day's events
tripped alarms in my wife's heart, which perhaps heightened her
feelings of temptation to read my manuscript pages without
asking for my permission (and knowing I wouldn't have given her
my permission), and now I do recall my wife was out in the studio
painting, *not* mowing the dandelions in the backyard. Needing
space to view some large photographs she'd clipped from magazines, she began cleaning off my desk space and doing so came
across my manuscript pages I'd carelessly (from her perspective,
arrogantly) left out in the open (and no, I didn't unconsciously

want my wife to catch me); add to that my wife's already feeling rejected because of the lack of emotional intimacy in our marriage, the way I was not really home when I was actually home, along with our issues around touch – me rarely touching her unless I believed it might tip us towards a nice fuck. So those feelings of rejection made reading my manuscript pages without asking me first not merely possible but necessary. Like: if there's a gas leak, call the gas company. Robert Walser's ardent walker-narrator refers to the space in which he writes as *his room of phantoms*. By phantoms, he means (I surmise) that darker and often secretive business of our lives – shameful acts and deeply rooted, unsatisfied desires, losses, regrets, smash-ups, trips never taken. In a craft essay about subtext, Charles Baxter asserts unthinkable thoughts threaten the very fabric of our existence. Reading my manuscript pages, my wife entered the dark room of her husband's phantoms: a pitch-dark, musty basement; low ceiling of splintery beams; old, defunct appliances hunched in corners; rusty nails scattered about the cold cement floor. It would be one thing if my wife were familiar with my phantoms, friends to them even, or one thing if we shared phantoms but we did not. Mine seemed to operate only in dreams while hers walked about the world. That is, she shared what she fixated on with me and at least two best friends although it would be naïve of me to think she didn't have thoughts or memories of experience or hopes (phantom hopes, dreams we cannot reconcile with our actuality) she couldn't share.

IN BED I told my wife I was thinking about leaving our marriage, that I felt our relationship had run its course and that my feelings for her, which were complicated but deflating and seemed only to generate kindness without intimacy, had reached their end, and she broke down crying, admitted that every day she worried about our marriage, already damaged with my dreams of Frannie and not helped by the fact I continued to write about all of this. Perhaps our marriage was irrevocably damaged, that is, we couldn't survive much longer. The next day she woke me up, said she felt sick to her stomach, asked me if I felt any hope for our marriage, for the rediscovery of intimacy and love we once shared (I could only remember wanting to fuck the dickens out of her), and I lied, I told her in a hesitant, strained voice (she had to pick up on this, had to see my little mouth) that I did want our marriage to succeed. These were my exact words: —I want our marriage *to succeed*. To describe our marriage with such reductive jargon – as if our marriage were a tenth-grade lab experiment! – revealed my true feelings about the future of our marriage. I did not want to be married. I did not want to leave my marriage. I did not have the courage to say, *I don't want you even though I once did. I have changed my mind.* Sometimes I think my unwillingness to break from our marriage was something more than fear (the fear of being alone-alone, the fear of an empty house, the fear of having to live with the knowledge I dissolved my family) that perhaps, beyond all of this knowledge of frumpy emotion, in the realm of mystery, of the half-known, existed a reason why our marriage was still intact and why in the face of its rapid dissolution I reached out to her. She asked me to tell her when I felt connected to her and I said, I feel connected to you right now, in your misery.

I SHARED WITH Frannie my shrink's number. My wife believed that my doing so had shattered the customer-barista boundary, and I guess she was right. Maybe my wife thought, Does that mean Frannie, this woman I don't even know, knows my husband is a depressive? Does this Frannie know (my wife thought) my husband struggles to be present when we're together? Doesn't my husband (my wife thought) have any sense of propriety or loyalty? Love? Does this Frannie know our marriage suffers? I should also mention my wife knew I didn't share my shrink's number with just anybody. Sometimes an acquaintance of mine, a student or co-worker say, asks me to recommend my shrink, which is like asking me if I can recommend mom as a surrogate parent. I lie. —No, she's not taking any new clients, I say. I don't want to inflict a stranger on my shrink. Said person doesn't deserve the insight and generosity my shrink offers. Said person doesn't deserve my shrink's varied selection of herbal teas and local coffees. Said person doesn't deserve the hugs she offers at the end of difficult sessions. Frannie more than deserved my shrink. Doesn't a caring friend share the phone number of his or her valued therapist? Again, my loyalty lay not with my wife but with Frannie, with my shrink. My wife, fork in hand, raked peas to her dinner plate's outer regions, away from fatty juices pooling around her pork chop. Her untouched pork chop. With her eyes cast down and lips clamped, her face expressed disgust and incredulity. —Frannie shouldn't be your friend, said my wife. —Frannie, said my wife, should be your barista. —But I write in the café five days a week, two hours per day, I said, —I cannot help but get to know the baristas personally. It's like we're co-workers, I said. I wished that were the truth. Seeing the pain in my wife's eyes (and hearing it in the tinny scraping sounds made by the fork sweeping across her dinner plate) I wished I were the husband she had in mind. Loyal husband. Doting husband. Husband who punctuated phone calls with an I love you. Husband whose inner life included *Desire for Wife*. The truth was I greatly admired my shrink. I wanted to gift (figuratively speaking) my shrink to Frannie because, well, I'd fallen for Frannie and when you fall for somebody, you give them your whole self. That is *the falling*. (My wife continued scraping her fork against the dinner plate.) You'd rip the nails off your toes for her, present her a daisy every week, make her mix CDs, snap Polaroids of all your favorite things you cannot show her, e.g., books, manual typewriter, dogs. You'd tuck said photographs in cards or tiny notes. You'd share your life in any way you could. For her you'd pass the name of your very reliable and compassionate, even poetic shrink. In inviting Frannie to see my therapist–this woman with whom I shared everything–I expressed my wish to share everything with Frannie, really, to extend this close intimacy to her, as

if, at the deepest of levels – of soul, of psyche – I wanted Frannie
and me to be the couple in counseling, not unlike the way my
expression of these particular thoughts in prose I intend to pub-
lish might be another way to destroy my marriage. Awakened
at dawn, I tried to focus my gaze on book spines and our chest of
drawers and the antique trunk next to our end table, all of which
appeared hollow and fragile, like stage props to a production
long-ago canceled. Then I saw Frannie and me taking every two
stairs to her apartment, me pawing at her. I try to be a trust-
worthy fellow. I can see how this memoir started out being about
one thing and has turned into something other. Kind of like life.
One day you love somebody desperately, madly and the next day
you ogle every woman who passes through the field of your
vision. You love her a little less without noticing it or you do notice
your feelings for her dwindle but it doesn't seem that important.
I do love my wife like one loves a sibling or an adequate traveling
companion one discovers late in life as a widower but I don't
love my wife like she loves me, I mean, I don't with any certainty
think, Yeah, I want to spend the rest of my life with her nor do
I think that about Frannie. OK, that's a lie, I do think that about
Frannie. My wife is not the kind of lover I want. She is not
another woman. She is not bold and unpredictable and volatile.
Not a screamer, not a frantic breather. She does not beg me
to shove my penis or two fingers inside her, to suck on her, to lick
her. She does not lap up. My wife's not the sloth-like, pack-a-day
depressive for whom I sometimes pine. She's a real doer. Yoga,
knitting, baking, keeping up with her girls. Choosing one woman
and that woman's unique characteristics closes off the possibility of loving another woman with different characteristics. That
seems a perfectly obvious assertion to make but it's not anything
I understood until I began to feel lonely inside my marriage.

THEY FUCK IN the unisex bathroom of the diner, they fuck in
the basement storage room, in the press box of the empty stadium, in the garage against the car, atop the car, in the backseat

and again in front seat, they fuck atop the riding mower, they
fuck in the stairwell between floors 18 and 19, between floors 34
and 35, in the janitor's closet, they fuck in cars and trucks and
minivans parked in otherwise empty parking lots of city parks
and universities and banks and big-box stores after hours and at
the end of dead-end streets, they fuck in paused elevator cars,
in toilet stalls of the men's and women's restrooms, they become
experts at seeking out spaces otherwise vacated, way off the
beaten-off path, remote, obscure as to be almost invisible, but not
invisible, that invisibility is an illusion, their illusion to share, we
cannot see through a wall, we cannot see what lies on the other
side of a tinted window, like a pocket inside a pocket of a pair of
skinny jeans bunched around her calves, this is not a story, this is
a meditation on simultaneity, on the plurality of space, physical
space, psychic space, concealing and opening up at the same time,
pushing your kid's stroller into her moist pussy, her sucking
and licking and lapping the lollipop he probably shouldn't let his
daughter have, that which is there, unseen and unheard, my
thoughts of her you cannot see, the narrow, twisting streets of the
Zizkov district in Praha continue to twist even as I write these
very words in Portland, in the home-team's dugout, atop the play
structure, anywhere they can they fuck, in motels, hotels, the unisex bathroom off the lobby of the Ace Hotel, they fuck in a
vacated office (door locked, blinds shut) next to a conference room
in which seven colleagues use language that means nothing, e.g.,
deliverables, sustainable, talking points, robust, they fuck to mean
something, the meaning of deep feeling, the meaning of precision and meaning *against* precision, of reaching for the person
reaching for you, the meaning of letting it go, of fucking because
we can, the orgasm unleashing sabotage and destruction, the
meaning of fucking it up badly while everybody else in that conference room restrains themselves from fucking one another,
in the stairwell between the top floor and the door to the roof, in
unused work rooms, board rooms unscheduled, they fuck in
bathrooms all over the world, *The Hole Room*, the room in which

we manage all our orificial leakages, emptying, leaving behind
our bodily excretions, our piss and shit and shreds of asparagus
between our teeth and bloody spit in a balled-up Kleenex and
Q-tips coated with ear wax and eye goop and soiled tampons and
semen beading down the inside of our thighs, O to fuck in the
room in which they towel off, O to wipe off, O to tidy and straighten
in front of the mirror, for maximum efficiency and ease of trans-
ition back into the world of plangent restraint, of scheduled
lunch breaks and spreadsheets projected on a screen, a big white
box boxing thousands of tiny boxes inside of which all the
numbers add up, precision in processes, prestige, exhaustion,
powering it up and down, pulling into *his* driveway, walking into
his house, O the illusory strength and comfort arising from the
illusion of house ownership, O *as if*, O brave fuckers, our deaths
are all we own, so splash a little water on your blushed skin
and on your stubble-burned cheeks, there in the fourth-floor restroom fucking, they are not where they are supposed to be and
later at home, away from each other, they are not where they are,
fucking each other in their thoughts, in memory, fucking in the
storage closet, the storage shed, an off-site storage space, a movable storage container parked outside her house, they fuck like
swifts fucking in flight, they fuck like sad adults fucking, with
tenderness and ardor and hostility for every fuck could be their
last, they might die of it, die of the fucking, they fuck out of the
loneliness they feel inside of their respective marriages, or
perhaps they do not know how to desire that which they do not
possess, together from a distance they dig a tunnel out of the
hole of feeling unknown or unrecognized by their spouses, out
of the hole of only seeing the self as alone in the world, O dumb
American life of marriage and children, O pick-up days of
Monday, Tuesday, and Wednesday, O *dalliance* that sounds like
eloquence and *penance* and *truculence*, O lovers enlivened by
the possibility of falling, we are together and separate, no, we are
together separate, no, we are separately together and the next day
burnt toast and cold cream and record shopping, but step

through the wall into existent invisibility, you are a superhero, you are a man, a woman, you are animals, in those fleeting moments of communion, of shared secrecy passed to and fro (like handball) they select each other and secrecy gives rise to the illusion of forever, hearing a whisper *above* the screaming, they select each other over everything else in the world, a choice that pushes back against American domesticity, a choice to have a choice, to choose what they cannot, to choose against what they once chose, to let go of love, to reach for what is off limits, to say one thing and do another, they fuck in the Avalanche Bar in Milwaukee, Wisconsin, they fuck in the National Liquor Bar in Milwaukee, Wisconsin, they do not want contentedness and dignity and safety, they do not want something that *runs well*, they do not want everything to be all right, they are fucking it up, they are fucking away from functionality into entangled feelings of misery and ecstasy, they want the glory hole and the great blue rod, they want to feel known not by their spouses but by *the other*, that which does and does not exist, he lies alone inside her heart as she does his, they fuck to obliterate what lies outside, they are lovers, they rub each other's temples, touch lightly each other's eyebrows, or no, they are not tender, they grip and squeeze and ram, they exact the thrilling punishment they feel they have deserved, they fuck because they love to fuck each other, she likes his rhythm (faster faster), the size of his penis (smaller), she lets him go down on her, he doesn't pull her up before he comes as her husband does, isn't ashamed of coming in her mouth, he loves the mess of sex, they try but fuck clumsily, their bodies don't fit together but they still fuck and fuck and fuck each other into late-summer's draining light, total ordinariness, a depression inside a depression, an unused room on an otherwise vacated floor, jammed stapler, foreclosed properties seized by banks along with other institutions make for very attractive proposals for purchasers, in the bathroom at the café, in the bathroom of Denny's, in their favorite bathroom at Little Big Burger, unisex and lock on the door and separated by a long hallway from the dining room, the red vinyl chair across from the toilet on which he sits her down and kneels before her pussy like a supplicant, like Mary Magdalene kneeling before Jesus to bathe his dirty feet, like two silly teenagers they fuck on the merry-go-round spinning in the pitch dark, on the smooth concrete bowl of the skate park beneath the bridge dividing the city between north and south, in the band's rehearsal space, in the recording studio, on the piano bench, his back smashing against the keys, O sweetly discordant music, O terribly wrong music, O birds of prey, O CEOs and CIOs and CFOs, may you once again take flight, may you never again mistake your own reflection for *the other*, smacking the mirrored glass and freefalling freefalling freefalling he moves inside her, the standing power fuck in a Porta-Potty, down three steep steps through the hatch under the deck into the berth, on top of the deck, they want to get as close as possible, to go as far as they can, to turn themselves inside out inside each other, they do not let their spouses hold them, they cannot be held so they fuck, in the bathroom of an Alaska Airlines MD-80 cruising at 30,000 feet, in the glass cockpit of Space Shuttle *Atlantis*, in the South Tower when that first plane hit, fucking in the face of death, fuck you, death, they fuck to feel alive in many different spaces at once, room 204 in the Comfort Inn near the airport or room 7 in Hotel Abalu in the Malasaña district of Madrid, the empty office, the empty passenger's side of the front seat, the fucking and the donefucking, how sexual feeling–the cock throb and the hmmmmm of clit–seem to pass *through* us, how the fucking seems over before it really is, before she comes, before he empties his semen inside of her behind her desk, beneath the cosmos outside a convenience store after close, history doth repeat itself, they fuck everywhere, O everywhere they fuck, except in the marriage bed, the line they cannot cross, not so much out of respect for respective spouses or partners but because to do so would be an admission they are killing something in the most cowardly of ways, there's no turning back, no illusion of marriage and domesticity and American cheerfulness to return to, an illusion inhabiting a psychic space and a real space, the space concealing a more truthful space, the fucking, the secrecy, the lying, one train may hide another, fucking in the marriage bed ruining the wonder (and illusion) of time-space plurality, man and wife talking in bed, *their* bed inside the house they own, God Bless Dumb America, the marriage sanctuary lovers need to destroy, to fulfill their own picture of cracked selfdom, you've gotta have something to fuck up, right, that's when I reach for my revolver, sometimes the only way to end a song is to smash the fuck out of your instruments, they fuck in a skyscraper, in every conceivable semi-concealed space simultaneously in every conceivable position, his pants around his ankles, hanging off only one ankle, hers balled up beneath or hanging on the hook on the back of the toilet stall door, her panties not even pulled off, just tugged aside at the crotch, in rooms only known to them, hidden from view, what we can never imagine, rooms we cannot see, airliners (United flight 175, American flight 11) piloted by terrorists bearing down at nearly 600 miles per hour on those towers full of fucking fuckers.

Tense

THOUGHT ABOUT YOU,
Think about you,
Will think about you.

Bring In the Clown

WHEN I'M ALONE, I DO SOME PRETTY WEIRD STUFF.
Like in the bathroom I make creepy faces in the mirror. I open my
mouth as wide as I can or scrunch my eyes or bite my lips, or I
shake my head as if I were having a palsied fit or nervous break-
down or I click my teeth to a Ramones' song or I puff up my
cheeks and widen my nostrils and slide my upper lip above my
gums to show my top teeth. Then I speak in wildly distorted
dialect. —That's the way I roll, I say in gangster speak. —Don't
bitch me, bitch, I say. Or in a exaggerated southern drawl, I say,
—Can you pour some of that bacon gravy over my home fries? Or
I break dance (without my cardboard!) on the bathroom tiles,
then I look at my reflection head-on and say, —*Bitch!* —You're a
moist bitch. —You're a collapsed house! —You're soggy white
bread! Then I pull my shirt over my head and hop around like
an inebriate bunny. Or in my best tyrant-boss-repressed-homo-
sexual-bully speak, I scream, —Where are my spreadsheets,
waste of sperm? —Can you reconcile the expense of my flaccid
penis? Later in the car, I flip off innocent drivers by looking
them in the eyes and saying, —Middle Finger. —Middle Finger.
Then I sing the douchebag song or I answer questions about this
book on *Fresh Air* or I rub my crotch as if it were my pussy. That's
right, I stroke my imaginary pussy, I say, —I like to eat my pussy,
Terry. Or I say in a measured and soft voice as if I were speaking
to a baby bunny whose bunny father is an inebriate, —I do not
want a dick in *my* anus but can I put mine in yours? I say things

that make no sense as if I were channeling another person's speech. —The colt delivers hiccup stares. Not stairs, *stares*. —Purple is plop. —No purple is plop locker. —Derelict moped moped. —You know, I used to be able to move my head back and forth. —Middle Finger. —Middle Finger. Then I gnash my teeth and slap the passenger's seat as if it were her buttocks. I love the word *buttocks*. Everybody: say it with me. *But-t-o-c-k-s*. I jut out my jaw, my bottom teeth rising over my top teeth, and I drive up I-5 north looking like Frankenstein, like a manmade monster everybody fears and nobody loves, till my gums and jaw begin to hurt. —Middle Finger. —Middle Finger. I moan in the way I want my wife to or I feign a choking fit, then I honk my horn and wave the other way. Like a worn-out mastiff whose name is Old Bear, I bark my disapproval of All Who Move. Arf. Arf. Arf. Arf. Arf. Arf. Arf. Arf. Arf. Arf. Arf. Arf. In an empty elevator car, I jump up and down or strut end to end like a runway model or the Rose Parade Queen atop a parade float, then I break into Voices Carry by 'Til Tuesday or I fake sneeze like five or six times super fast, I rub my crotch against the mirrored panel to get as close to my reflection as is humanly possible.

The Manuscript (IV)

IN BED I BEGAN TICKLING MY WIFE'S NAVEL. FOREPLAY.
She held my hand away from her breasts from which our son
had just fed. Our son changed irrevocably the ways in which my
wife and I related to each other. My wife not only found a male
creature on whom to shower her love but she was on the receiving
end of a particular, intense love, a baby's unfettered love (comprised of absolute need, physical and emotional), a love more
passionate and primal and accepting than any husband love. With
the roles of lover and beloved filled, I moved into the role
of protector. I became the janitor, chef, personal assistant, dog
walker. At night I switched off lights and shut down the house.
I was necessary yet peripheral. When our son slept and my wife
and I could take a moment to ourselves, we did so rarely or if
we did, we spoke about our jobs like exhausted servers between
shifts. In this new role I could fulfill my wife with busy work and
with a modicum of conversation. During those sleep-deprived
autumnal months (when your part of the golden-lit earth tilts
towards darkness) after your first child is born and as your wife
and baby bond outer-womb and your Superman-self brushes
up against a deafening domestic quietude (diapers, tiny socks,
dryer sheets), you might feel tempted to cheat on your wife, to
follow a woman who has no child to bear, who wants only to fuck
you. It's easier than you think to slip out the back door. I'm
reminded of the Raymond Carver short story, "The Father," in
which the children, mother, and grandmother crowd around the

newborn baby. Turned away from his family, the father sits at
the kitchen table. In figuring out whom the baby resembles the
most – mother or father – the older children decide the father
doesn't resemble anybody in the family. Carver describes the
father's face as *white and without expression*. A face without expression is not a face. Today I ask my son what he wants for lunch.
He says he wants eggs. He says he wants eggs the way I always
cook eggs. Despite my need for solitude and my enormous struggle to be present in the company of my family, despite the
knowledge I'm a decent father, a sufficient father (although I
could be so much better if I weren't so distracted by my thoughts),
a better father than dad was to me, in that moment when my son
says, *the way you always cook them,* I can't think of anything
better I have done or am doing or will ever do than raise my son.
He knows exactly how I prepare his eggs and in turn I feel known
in a way that is mysterious to me (to me I'm unrecognizable –
who is this father creature?) yet I feel the strong and meaningful
impact I have on my son. I imagine all the people in the future –
lovers, friends, his children – for whom he will prepare eggs, and
in his own way.

I STOPPED WRITING at the café to be at home with my son in
the afternoons. During his naps, lasting anywhere from 20 minutes to three hours, I'd steal away to the garage-turned-studio to
write and after my son woke up, I'd make him a little snack and
we'd go for a walk around the neighborhood or play in the driveway, or if he wasn't feeling well, we'd watch *Sesame Street* On
Demand. As a deeper love for my son took root, I became more
focused on my wife, which is to say, I was less disposed to dream
about Frannie and to think that some other, better life separate
from my own awaited me. What waited for me – no matter what
choice I made – was more heartbreak and loneliness. Despair.
Emptiness. My therapist (individual) showed me a photograph of
a sculpture in which the father embraces the mother holding
their baby. The artist distorted the figures to appear unreal. Their

shoulders are impossibly broad and bowed and their shrunken heads have no distinct facial features, perhaps placing emphasis on the family relationship – away from the individual with distinct soul. Forms we fill with our lives. Stepping lightly so as not to wake the baby. Not missing each other when we should. Work calling. Then my shrink handed me a newspaper clipping about an archaeological dig in Egypt in which scientists dug up human remains in that exact pose: father nesting mother nesting baby. Imagine a disaster (devastating wind storms or catastrophic earthquakes) around 500 B C in which mother urgently cradles her crying baby (baby scared because limestone walls shake and slide, then split) and the father scrambles over to shelter both mother and baby against falling debris. Notice how father protects wife-mother and baby simultaneously. That is, when the father embraces one, he cannot help but embrace the other, for a mother and her baby for many years are one. Our son looked like my wife: blue eyes and pallid skin and curly blond hair. Yesterday I raised strawberry ice cream to my son's mouth and recognized in his upward glance (its tentative anticipation) a look my wife gets when she needs a hug at the end of a long day. Mine and my wife's post-coitus conversation often turns to our son. In James Salter's *Light Years*, the omniscient narrator says (of Viri and Nedra): *Their life was two things: it was life, more or less – at least it was the preparation for one – and it was the illustration of life for their children. They had never expressed this to one another, but they were agreed upon it, and these two versions were entwined somehow so that one being hidden, the other was revealed. They wanted their children, in those years, to have the impossible, not in the sense of the unachievable but in the sense of the pure.* All on his own my son tugs the yellow chord, signaling the bus to stop. —Stop bus, stop, he says. Arriving home our son runs in the entryway, screams, —Come say hello to mommy. She's in the kitchen. Come in, come say hello, and I do as my son says.

BUT WHO PROTECTS the father?

I OFTEN IMAGINE my wife's death. By car accident. Or maybe she's riding her ten-speed home from work and a car, some assfuck speaking on his cellphone, drives into my wife, throwing her off her bike and into a brick building or an oncoming car. Imagine a knock at the front door and the dogs leaping off the couch, barking and my son, mimicking the dogs, barking. Cracking the door, I find two police officers whose somber eyelids and lips in-sucked portend grave bodily harm. Skull collapse, gnarled cartilage. A bag of groceries spilled over the center lane. I step out on the stoop and close the door behind me. They say it. They tell me as if we're the ones letting go of our souls. Malta! Malta! Inside the house, my son's face crumples as he asks, —Where's my mommy? Presently, as I type, she's in the next room watching reality television while knitting a sweater for our niece. If my wife were to die, I'd lament the paintings not painted and gifts never bought or received and socks and slippers filled by other feet and stone pavers cold against those other feet, now bare. Our young son, just old enough to speak in complete sentences, as in, I don't know, or When are you going to wake up?, would grow up without a memory of his mother. He'd often say, *Tell me a story about mom.* Or maybe he'd never speak with me about his mother but instead hold labyrinthine conversations with her ghost inside his thoughts while in the car, showering, riding an empty elevator to the tenth floor, or perhaps he'd feel her love and protection combined with a vertiginous loss, loneliness too, whenever he'd smell lavender or wet grass and topsoil or swing open the door to the café or hear her favorite Bob Dylan song or touch the scratchy, heated surface of a just-used dryer sheet. Her love for our son, another way to say, the way she knows our son, would die right along with her body. As the police officers play with my son (*Would you like to hold my badge?*), I telephone my wife's parents and then our best friend and I'm still crying but not letting on that I stopped loving my wife, which makes me cry harder and love her more because she didn't die loved by me. That's right, I pity-loved her. I know if she was alive (and she is, ironing work clothes for the next day), she'd hate my pity and later that night after the police leave and our friend comes over to help with my son, I call the funeral home, talk to somebody about cremation options or maybe the policemen drive me to the morgue to identify the body. Does that actually happen or is that just on TV? Jump to the post-funeral reception where women are attracted to sad-me in the kitchen filling the tea kettle or sorting crackers and cheese and salami slices on a serving dish (my wife's favorite snack). The women think, He'd be a good catch. Good looking, generous enough, a sense of humor definitely. Or: His wife always said he's particularly talented in bed, that he loved to go (and stay) down on her. I know such a fantasy fails to capture anything ordinary let alone the grief and anger and loneliness I would feel if my wife actually did die but imagine new lovers whose cheeks touch and stay touching. On the breakfast table a bowlful of cold purple grapes. A few months after the funeral I'm soaking in the bathtub, smoking, tapping ashes into a heavy glass tray on the linoleum floor peeling up at the edges, the floor my wife and I planned on replacing with Aztec Tiger Marmoleum, a dazzling, durable floor, a floor that unlike me gives a little with each step. I sit in the bath and stare at my jagged, sallow toenails. My dogs doze on the couch, my son's down for the night. (In fantasy small children always sleep so soundly.) A knock at the door. I'm unshaven, unwashed, my hair gummy. I'm holed up. Admittedly I wouldn't miss the way the telephone rings nonstop, every call for her. The few friends I have are the kind of friends who, like me, hate to speak on the telephone. They never call. Even if the caller ID identifies the caller as a friend of mine, my wife still picks up and chats for a few minutes before handing – no, not handing – raising the hand cradle to my ear even though I have requested she let the call go to voicemail, or if she has to answer, tell whomever it is I'm not home. I'm a curmudgeon. I don't know what happened to me. One night I fell asleep a social, debaucherous, healthily unhealthy young man and woke up a cantankerous grandpa who prefers not to leave the house or talk to anybody. I wonder if this tunnel life of mine is the result of endless yearning for a woman whose face I cannot touch to mine, like I cannot drive more than one automobile, nor can I hide in the woods behind my parents' house and not because my parents are divorced and no longer live in that house and not because my parent's house only exists in my thoughts but because the woods I remember are in Indiana and I'm in Portland. Marrying one woman. Another knock. I rise from the gray tepid water, slip into a thin robe. Light another cigarette in case I feel like blowing smoke in some solicitor's face. You can never blow enough smoke in a solicitor's face. At the door is Frannie in a brown sleeveless dress with ruffled skirt and dirty canvas shoes. Her sandy hair tossed-up in a hurry is not at odds with her carefully painted lips. —Riot red, she says in the kitchen, making coffee for both of us (opening four drawers before she finds a spoon) and we discuss books or we don't talk at all, just sit across from each other listening to my son's breathing or the bath water draining or we take the dogs and my son for a much-needed walk to Alberta Park or maybe Frannie tucks a strand of her hair behind her ear and takes the chewing gum from her mouth (setting it on the oil cloth covering the table) and we kiss and later, after my son is down, we have sex, not an erotic production but tender and sad, a faint, solid clap of our bodies. Or I lick her down there. Or I tousle strands of mussed hair. Or I trace swooping lines over the sharp curves of her buttocks, her hipbone shaped like a scythe. I wish for this moment to protract like a darkened hotel room of late afternoon, curtains drawn and bed unmade, the outside world a snowfall in another city. I'm touching the skin I thought impossible to touch and loving the battered soul I thought impossible to love. *Here's to you, Mrs. Robinson, Jesus loves you more than you will know.* I guess I'm not used to living anywhere but inside my thoughts, which is to say, I'm living in the past or in some oblique fantasy-future, never the present with my wife knitting a garment that will warm the skin and blood of a child, knitting steadily like a supplicant who lights candles for her sins and for the sins of other sinners. May my wife be delivered from me. On her way to the door, Frannie says she'd like to come over again. She doesn't say, *I'm worried about you*. My wife does that, says, *I'm worried about you*, says, *You smoke too much*, says, her ear to my chest, *Your heartbeat is way too fast*. My fantasy-dead wife copes with the emptiness of sharing a bed with a zombie-husband by making plans, by orchestrating the radiant, discordant music of our lives (*Let's get out of the house, finally* or *Shouldn't you call your mom today?* Or *Why don't you run this afternoon*). Schemes and events and projects that erect for my wife an illusion of pleasant, mindful togetherness. The family wheel. Strap your son in the swing and push gently. I'm saying my sadness has no home in our home. On the phone with a friend, my wife says, *That's so cute*. And, *I'm so happy for you guys*. Her tone grates. Frannie would never fill the silence with hollow, cheerful chatter. Frannie's reticent, at ease with (or, like me, in awe of) demons that draw her away from the world. When the telephone rings, Frannie continues smoking and says nothing. Probably scarring. Frannie finds the paragraph where she left off and continues. Frannie plays the melancholy music of Astor Piazzola or Tom Waits or Doug Shepard. Frannie does all the stuff my wife doesn't. Frannie exists only in my carpenter-ant thoughts. If my wife were to die, I wouldn't miss her the way a lover misses his beloved. My wife, dead, wouldn't haunt me. In crowds I wouldn't see her face nor would I in the night reach out for her little-girl's hand and wrist. I wouldn't imagine her sitting across from me at the dinner table, lifting forkfuls of sticky rice to her mouth. I wouldn't dream her up the way a widower needs his deceased wife to somehow touch him or speak to him, even the slightest sound, a sound routinely shared in their marriage, comforting him, like knuckles cracking or the dog's overgrown toenails clicking against the hardwoods. The bath water appears to be draining very slowly. Who's to say how I'd react to my wife's death? Perhaps I will die first. The last person to ask is the author. Perhaps it seems I have not lived so closely to a dying creature breathing its final breaths and have not watched the surface of a dying face closed off to the living and have not witnessed deep physical suffering followed by the slow letting go of that suffering, the fight not to let go, the fight against human weakness. Death doth not create fucking, death creates death. Although how easy it is to imagine slipping away, taking her to a public restroom or driving her to an empty parking lot and fucking her till you come inside her, I mean, you're standing on some massive burial ground, bearing witness to another lost human body interred but wanting nothing more than to part with slow tongue the wet labia of the woman standing across from you next to the attending priest sprinkling holy water atop the casket. *O wet pussy, I pray / for you. Through you, we come / into life, into its fleeting / bloom, its slowly beautiful (painful) decay.* I was a little boy, now I am not. Living is an erratic interval between two points that do not exist. I will always feel like the little boy I no longer am. We push off against death towards death. What else is there besides fucking and death? Books. To touch your parched lips and then the tip of your tongue to her pussy is to forgive death for its pressing for-ward. Love is separate. I kindly ask you to remove your shirt and bra and lift your skirt and feel in the shadows with slippery fingers for what is extant and unapparent, for what is plausible, for potentiality, the possibility of *the fill*. Who among us lives among the living and among the dead? Seeking my attention, my son throws a ball at my face. This dream, or this consideration of a dream, is not so much a wish for my wife's death, no, I wish for my wife a long life filled with beauty and meaning, I wish for my wife to be loved more than I love (or do not love) her at this present moment of composition. (For me, it is always about the present moment of composition.) Perhaps this making is another way to escape another kind of dream that is more prob-able: the seemingly everlasting crushing pummel of adultery or the muck and fire of an extended separation then drafty divorce. Our lives are ruins. Perhaps one kind of dream sets aside or avoids while another seems to test out more likely possibilities,

the plotting of X and Y. This is an extrapolation, the plotting of
points unplotted. Do I want my wife to die? No, I do not. Do I want
Frannie to remove her clothes and join me in the bathtub? Yes,
I do. If I feel so separate from my wife's love, why do I continue to
reach out for her? Walking from work to our son's preschool, I
flip open my cellphone and call my wife. I have nothing to say, I'm
not missing her, it's a habit, I run my fingertip across the groove
of our attachment. I say, *I'm on my way to pick up our son*. I say,
Should I run to the grocery store on the way home? Wait for the call, an
ex-girlfriend whom I still to this day fantasy-finger-fuck once
said to me in response to my question, *Should we hang out more?*
Driving home with ice cream, I call my wife. Leave a message.
From the backseat my son asks, *Why did you call mommy?* And I
say, *Why, son, why do I call her?* And he says, *Because she answers*.
Because she answers. Because the sound of her voice comforts me
but comfort disappears when I do not hear the voice after which
I pine. I don't tell my wife any silly stories from my day. I don't say,
I'm sad. I don't tell her the knock-knock joke Frannie emailed
me. *Knock knock. Who's there? We? We Who? We-are-not-intrepid*.
My inner life of which my wife is not a part. Two parts whiskey,
one part glass. My wife refuses to read sad books. That's depress-
ing, she says. No, I say, I'm a depressed person, the story makes
you feel sad. She asks, How does it make you feel? I say, Like a cozy
yellow light from a bedside lamp. Why not imagine a divorce?
Why not ask my wife for a divorce? Because those scenarios, real
or imagined, involve me setting fire to this shabby house I've
helped to build. I mean, even though I'm attracted to my wife and
enjoy our sex-making of the rougher variety, though rarely it is,
and even though we are companions to each other, buddies we
are, my wife repels me. My body does not soften but tenses to
her touch. My body says, Leave me alone, leave me to my inside
place. I do not want my body to say this and sometimes I tell it not
to, force it to say other things, such as, OK, time to touch you so
that you my wife can feel loved in this life. Who really wants to fantasize conflict, who wants to dream up a wallowing confession?

Perhaps I'm waiting for my wife to leave me, that is, I'm too cowardly, too afraid to leave her and my son, too afraid to disappoint
them, too afraid to be alone, too afraid to live alone with the
knowledge I hurt other human beings, I hurt my wife, I hurt my
son, I fail at marriage and at family, and what's worse is how
I take for granted my wife's seemingly indefatigable devotion to
our marriage (look out the porthole at the endless ocean), as if
her devotion, which includes her capacity for forgiveness, were
somehow infinite and not being gnawed on and worn away by
these very words that are separate from my wife, these words
potentially, irrevocably hurtful to her, these words revealing my
distorted version of our private lives, my state of mind lost
inside an American marriage. Perhaps I write out of a repressed
desire to pulverize what remains of our marriage. Perhaps my
writing this manuscript forces my wife into a place where she has
no choice but to serve *me* papers like the wife who so decisively
serves her husband divorce papers (Snap! Hand clap! No flap!)
the very day she verifies the evidence – examining his cellphone
records, calls received, calls made, calls missed – of her husband's
affair. Am I offering my wife *a record to verify the evidence*? Is my
writing the manuscript simply a cruel act of passive aggression?
Sometimes the last person in the world to ask is the author.
Peer through the looking glass at Frannie raising her brown dress
over her head, see Frannie's finger dipping into her underpants.
More scarring. I pluck the petal of my wife (that is my wife), and
then I grow angry at me for not loving or leaving her, and I grow
angry at her for not leaving me, for staying put, and she's angry at
me for rejecting her, for not shitting and not getting off the pot,
and our anger mixes together, our anger fucks very hard, and
afterwards she dreams of ice-fingers groping her, of house parties
at which she drinks from an empty, finger-smudged glass,
watching me leave with another woman. Imagine a mist that soaks
the bones cold. Imagine a board game with its torn lid stacked
beneath piles of decade-old *Time* magazines in the basement of
a house in which boys, now grown up, no longer live. Now imagine

the mother, upstairs, sitting alone at the kitchen table. *Because she answers*. My wife and I, we are not unkind to each other. Imagine Frannie's cheek brushing mine, hovering there like a hand poised to cover another. I mean, if my wife were to die by car accident or if we were to divorce, I'd still see her face in my son's slight lips and blue eyes and pallid skin and his curly blond hair. My wife and I linked forever through the little soul of our dear son. I can never leave her even when I do and I do, I leave her every day in my thoughts.

WHAT MOMMY SAYS to daddy: If I had a dick I'd come too.

WHEN I'M ALONE I spend half my time dreaming of being with strangers, yearning for their touch. I'm animal-prone to mate with another, to touch and be touched by that elusive other. I want to be here with you. Here I am. Outside of that desire I can enjoy the company of other people yet after a while I feel antsy, outside of self, unhinged, without sound or feeling and I over-compensate through excessive chat or brooding reticence. Inside my head, I set fire to the woods behind my childhood home, I erase entire alphabets from the flimsy walls of our days. I lose sense of beauty, of wonder, of sadness, of loss, of the death in our lives, of the ghosts passing through my thoughts, my grand-father picking me up from winter practice in his bright orange pick-up and then the drive through fields, frozen and fallow. I need to reel myself back in, to self-slowness where I can feel, where I can live again. Dreaming awake is the way I experience the particular and writing is one way I can dream awake. We lie down on the blanket and Frannie tents open the waistband of her underpants (*Call them panties*, she says) beneath which spat-ters rust-orange curlicues (all those lowercase "c"s!) nesting around her pubic bone. She positions my hand above her crotch, says, *Keep your hand poised at the center of desire that lies just outside my pussy*.—Why not yearn for what you actually have in your hands? —Because I'm afraid to go deep. Living alone is a way of being in this world. When I listen to music through headphones the song is for me only. What's being pumped into my conscious-ness is yearning that moves me from one moment to the next and satisfying that yearning means living with somebody else, which is not what I want, what I want is you, lay your ear against the tabletop and listen for my heartbeat.

I CAN LOVE not her but memory of her.

I HAVE NO qualms about taking me, us – me, my wife, my son – into debt. If there is a book I want, if it is morning, afternoon, or evening and I want a latte, if I don't have enough money in my account to fill up my tank, I will, without a second thought, pay with my credit card. I used to do all of our bills so it was pretty easy for me to hide our credit card debt from my wife. Then I ran the card up to like $4K and after I finally told her, after a lot of screaming and tears, I stopped doing the bills and cut up my credit card because I couldn't trust myself to only use it for emergencies. Now I have a credit card again and I can't be trusted to only use it for emergencies. I do not save money. I cannot spend within my means (as the experts say). We have tried all kinds of solutions. We have combined accounts, separated accounts, made separate accounts for bills and spending, loaded accounting software on our computer, kept and tracked ALL receipts, discussed solutions with financial planners, with our therapist, with my therapist, with my psychiatric nurse. None of it seems to work. I make a commitment to a new solution but then I bounce a check or use my credit cards for books and coffee. I easily convince myself I have to have a book, I have to have a latte. I say something to myself like you need to get this book now, today, it has something relevant to say to you today, you need to incorporate this book into the work you're doing, or this book is going to garner much, much acclaim, underground acclaim of course, although no book I love these days seems to garner any-thing but underground acclaim or no acclaim, but perhaps

its first print run will sell out, so I MUST have the first edition, I
must show others I knew about this book first, I contributed
to its acclaim, I'm the sole reason for its acclaim, I'm special, you
are special, I say to myself. My wife suggested when I find myself
in this situation, when I'm buying something to buoy some
aggrandized illusion of self, think of her, imagine her frustration,
and I do, I imagine my wife's disappointment, her thinning eyes
and her top teeth biting into her bottom lip, but I dismiss swiftly
that picture of her in pain as I'm hurting her, I say to myself,
I will tell her it's a gift for my father or mother, which is to say, I
make up a lie (ridiculous) and I buy the book and afterwards I
fill with shame and anger, for I've done exactly what I said I would
not do, and what's worse I direct that anger at my wife. She comes
to me for a hug or a kiss or touches my hand, wants to make a
brief connection, and I recoil, I try to move around the hug, I push
her away. I wrongly blame her. I freak out because she hasn't filled
the dogs' water bowl or switched the laundry. I think, I wouldn't
feel so ashamed or angry if she didn't insist I spend within my
means, if she were more flexible, if she didn't deem my behavior
as mistaken, if she were not so disappointed in me (other women
would not be so disappointed in me), I wouldn't feel so angry
at myself and I would have what I want, my books and my lattes,
two or three a day sometimes (why can't I just stick with one
a day?), and it's not just the lattes but the experience of sitting at
cafes with strangers, the possibility of a fuckable woman in
view (right now a fuckable woman is in view!), I can't write in my
office at home, can't settle for making coffee in my kitchen, I
have to write at a café so I can be connected to the nipple, the tit,
the teat of lustrous illusion, that I might get to fuck one of these
fuckable women in view, that I might dazzle one of these strange
women with my Stupendous Selfness!, with my emotive speak!,
or more simply I like to look at these fuckable women, their bodies,
no need to go further on this point (dumb useless antidote to
loneliness, to difficulty), the point being my overspending is
directly connected to this picture I have of myself alone and to my

desire to live separate from my wife. To live in books, in dreams of books, dreams of other women, other lives, other pages, of frothy steamed milk. I cannot, to use my therapist's language (couples), partner my wife in her need to stay not only financially afloat but somewhat comfortable (as comfortable as two teachers can be). I'm not there for her. Sure, I'm there with her in therapy, on the white leather couch (Ikea?) of our therapist, to admit my wrongdoings and to make new plans, better plans, there have been so many new, better plans, I'm there for her in that moment, that is, I want her to be supported and I want to be the person to support her but when we go our own ways, I have no interest in being that person she wants me to be or I only want to be that person not because I actually want to be that person but because I want to stop feeling ashamed, I want to stop hating myself and misdirecting my anger at her, I don't want my son to have to bear witness to my anger, to the way my shame fuels my anger and my capacity to direct that anger towards others who do not deserve to witness it or hold it, to not coat my son with male rage. I want to show my son that ordinary disappointment is not an abnormal psychic state, does not have to give rise to shame and self-hatred, I do not want to teach my son how to hate himself, please, God, let my son not take that from me if he hasn't already, yet me wants what me wants, I want this book and the writing of this book (this present moment) that momentarily makes me feel less alone in the world, and special too like I'm chosen, and I want this coffee (latte) in this café where I can pine after Frannie who sits across from me, I can take in her body I do not possess, will never possess, will never be held by, her body by which I want not to be held, don't touch me.

IN THERAPY (COUPLES), I admitted to my wife I'd been dreaming about Frannie again. The Frannie part was unimportant, I stupidly believed; what mattered (I thought) was the dynamic my dreams portrayed, the way this other woman and I related to each other, the way we shared our broken joys and

picked at each other's scabs. —Frannie-Smannie, I said, a lie, and
with half a couch cushion separating us, my wife stared at me,
her eyes stretched by anger and disorientation and the office's dry
air. Skin lotion was passed. My wife suggested I scoot closer but
sitting close to her would feel (to me) disingenuous, as if we were
trying to impress our therapist with a couch cuddle. My wife
said, —I thought you were done with these dreams. —Apparently
not, I said. —Apparently not, she repeated. —What's going on
in that fucking skull of years? My wife asked, her fingertip tapping
my forehead, tap, tap, door-knocking a house whose lone occu-
pant, unbeknownst to her, stood next to her on the front porch on
the wrong side of the locked door, the key to that door lost forever.
They'd never get inside, those two. Our therapist interrupted:
—You can stop fingerbeating your husband now, and my wife with-
drew her hand but its incredulous index finger continued
pumping back and forth, the clock ticking closer to the end of our
session. Death does not part us, love does. —This realization is
helpful, it explains why we're growing apart. —And why is that?
She asked. —Because you're not showing me your broken stuff,
I said. —You're breaking my stuff right now, she said. I should
have touched her hand, stilled her ticking finger, scooted over
closer to her and even now, writing this, I think, if my love for
my wife weren't so shallow, then my prose might reflect that, that
is I might be more generous in my descriptions of my wife but
I'm not that writer and not that husband. With my arms crossed,
still seated a good half-cushion from my wife's leg folded under,
I lied. Not: *I don't love you enough to remain married to you.* Not:
I love somebody else more than you. I continued to lie to my wife at
couples therapy. The matter was sufficiently unsettled. I deflected
our problems onto my wife.

PRESENTLY MY WIFE obsesses over wounded birds–juncos,
hummingbirds, thrush, jays, crows–she finds in the backyard.
She layers newspaper and twigs and grass blades and kale in
a shoebox and places the delicate bird in its new nest. Every few

hours, she drips sugar water through a needleless syringe into its mouth. (We have to do a better job at caring for each other. For us. For our son.) Often the bird's wounds heal and it walks or flies away or she drives it to our local Audubon Society for more intensive care, but if it dies, she brings its body into our studio and paints it. Her depictions emphasize through distortion of shape and jarring color combinations the wound. Broken blood feathers, puncture marks in breast, blood dribbling from toe-nails. Our garage studio is filled with paintings of dead birds. She sees dead birds in a way she's never seen them and she paints what she sees: dead birds lying on their backs, beaks tipped to sky through which they no longer fly, blood pooling below toenails in a nest of charred nettles.

The Saddest Part of the Story

THEN CAME MY TURN TO LEAVE FOR COLLEGE IN MILWAU-
kee where my middle brother already lived. The plan was to
meet up at the dorm. Dad's Olds pulled up to Schroeder Hall and
sitting on a park bench next to my middle brother was the
oldest who'd flown back to Milwaukee from the Bay Area. I like to
think my older brothers recognized how difficult my leaving
home would be for mom: before she returns to that nearly empty
house in the woods, my brothers thought, let her have a weekend
with her three boys. Little did any of us know dad was planning
his escape, the grand finale. I mean to say, this was our last weekend together, as a family. I mean to say, I was unaware our time
together this weekend would be the sort of thing I'd want to recall.
Sometimes one wants to watch his lover walk out of his life
forever. I do imagine, probably that first night, a Friday night, all
of us would've gone to Sal's, an Italian restaurant dad liked. Sal,
the owner, was a friend of a friend and dad liked to know and be
known by owners. He and Sal acted like best pals, they clapped
each other on the back, called each other *Paisano. —Hey, Paisano.*
At Sal's we ate pasta, *family style. Family style* means we ate from
a single platter. *Family style* means we served ourselves. I wish
I'd taken notice of where we were seated and what the placemats
looked like (paper ones with maps of Italy and Sicily and bad
photography of Roman ruins) and the delight on mom's face, all
her boys with her when we no longer needed her. We could not
see ahead yet leapt forward into the thicket. I would've observed

the way mom and dad tippytoed around feelings of resentment
and despair, mom drinking more than eating, Sal refilling her
glass, dad overcompensating for the recoil he felt by patting mom's
shoulder or laughing a little too hard at mom's anecdote about
the dog licking air. And what about the dog, where was the dog?
In the house in the woods (in the house no longer a house), the
dog snoozed on the couch, awaiting the white-haired two-legged
to arrive with dry kibble and belly scratches. Not wanting to flap
her hip-yelp or gleep her throat glob, the dog greeted two-
leggeds from the couch. I wish I could remember thinking, How
lonely you must feel, dad. Did your heart whistle for another
woman? Did you dream of her tickling your neck below the hair-
line or holding your hand under the table or leaning her head
against your shoulder or tracing faint lines over your shut eyelids?
I would've paid close attention to whether or not we'd cleaned
our plates, would've felt consoled on the drive back to my dorm-
itory by the routine way we arranged ourselves in the car: dad
driving and mom shotgun and us boys in the backseat, me
squished in between my older brothers. I didn't imagine mom on
the drive back to Indiana, crying or not crying, peering out the
window at flat harvested fields, dad senselessly fiddling with radio
knobs, in his thoughts, asking mom for a divorce. I slammed
cheap beer and smoked weed and swallowed shots of whatever
my new friends poured me. I sang along to R.E.M.'s "It's the End
of the World As We Know It (and I Feel Fine)." It was the end of
my world, that house no longer a house. After bong hits, cigarettes,
a greasy, diner breakfast of fried eggs, hash browns, and sausage
links, and more cigarettes, I fucking felt fine. It was late August
of 1989, a few months before the Berlin Wall was to fall. *The Wall
is down, The Wall is Dead.* I remember R.E.M.'s music video
for that song, the trashed and gutted house strewn with garbage,
chunks of drywall, old magazines once glossy with crisp pages
now faded and wrinkled and torn, furniture turned upside down.
A young teenage boy, shirtless, rummaging through debris, tearing pages, pilfering cupboards and drawers, discovers a black

and white photo of a man, circa late 19th century, a man wearing a bowler hat, his tight skin and flat lips suggesting solemnity and fastidiousness, his soaked eyes revealing physical exhaustion, despair, the indefatigable tapping of duty and misfortune, like Job, like the bell's peal, a man who feeds his brothers and sisters before himself, and a hundred years later, a photo of this man held to the chest by a boy in another house no longer a house, a boy posing in front of a film camera, like a still shot, the boy still, the man in the photo the boy holds still, one time transposed on another, then the moment slips away the way one day mom and dad, now divorced, sign papers and the house in the woods begins to disappear from my family's consciousness, the way my son one day stops riding in a stroller. Picking up skateboard, the boy in the abandoned house practices front and backsides, kickflips, his skateboard clapping the warped, rotting hardwood floors, behind him a missing wall section looking out onto weeping willows and wisteria, summer's swarm of crickets scratching their legs, the boy who deeply enjoys the squalor upon which he's happened and the brokenness of things, the way broken things exist in this life.

I THINK OF our old house as an actual house, its exterior stained twig-brown, the whole thing nestled in woods like my little son in a sleeping bag, and on the top floor of the house (no longer a house), I see dad standing at his dresser in white v-neck undershirt dabbed with pit stains, white boxer shorts, black over-the-calf socks, emptying loose change into an ashtray no longer used to collect ashes. He rubs his eyes as if pushing back against the worry of his heavy thoughts. For every task he completes, another ten appear. In dreams he sprints in crowded packs of runners throwing elbows. On the main floor next to the kitchen where dad's dinner stays warm in the oven sit mom and me and the dog curled up at mom's feet, passing gas. We tune the TV to *M*A*S*H*, and beneath us in the basement, the ID of our house, my brothers laugh as they sneak sips of whiskey or dry-hump girls, the pinball machine lit up like the big city at night in which none of us yet live, the silver ball smacking bumpers and popping bells. Flick your boogers any fucking place you want.

AFTER COLLEGE (MIDDLE '90s) I lived in a studio apartment. My books neatly lined a built-in case next to the only window looking out onto Wisconsin Avenue as it passed through campus towards Milwaukee's drab financial district. Other than books, largely novels and story and poetry collections, I owned very little: clothes and a futon and some kitchen supplies and a laptop computer for my writing. Upon graduation I'd trashed my notebooks and folders and sold back all textbooks. My friends had moved on to entry-level jobs that paid handsome enough salaries and offered full benefits. I had no benefits, didn't want them. The entry-level-job lifestyle seemed too grown-up for me. Too menial. I could sense the quiet depravity our corporate culture radiated, always rewarding scheming and striving at all costs while belittling contemplation and generosity of feeling. I stayed on campus, working part-time at the university bookstore and bartending a couple nights a week at an east-side dive serving underage drinkers. My days were easy. I'd masturbate whenever I felt like it. Living alone freed me up. When I had roommates, there was always the fear one of them might catch me beating off. So I'd hide away in my bedroom or the bathroom and play music or run water in order to drown out any sounds that might suggest to my roommates I was masturbating. In a shared living situation, a shut door screamed, *Please don't come in because I'm masturbating*. It wasn't much fun pleasuring myself as my roommate swept the hallway hardwoods or brushed his or her teeth in the adjoining bathroom. Living alone allowed me to engage in theatrics. Minor theatrics, I should say. I'd slowly undress, then lift the case around my pillow as if I were raising a woman's skirt. I'd whisper nasty little secrets to the crumpled bedsheets, plunge a probing finger in the thin mattress. This all felt very real to me to the extent interactions with actual people –

co-workers, regulars, whomever – felt more like dreams in which people's faces became effaced and the ground beneath could disappear at any moment. Through the east wall I could hear the shower running in the bathroom of the apartment next to mine and the voices of its two female inhabitants, college students. They spoke loud enough to be heard over the sound of spraying water. I imagined one at the sink, plucking her eyebrows or rolling on deodorant and the other in the shower, rubbing soap into a lather. Their favorite topic of conversation was sex. Methods, positions, equipment, unusual occurrences. One day I heard the first woman say, —He likes to sixty-nine, the other, —You're so vulgar. —OK, so what do you call it? —Doug and I, the other said, —Give *each other oral pleasures*. This conversation immediately turned me on and I masturbated on the spot. I liked the verb *give*: sex as a gift, not necessarily perverse (although it could be, who was I to judge?) but generous, as in *this is something you would like so I will give it to you*. On occasion I heard through the east wall high-pitched sex screams and boy grunts. At some point one of these women had knocked on my door. I wasn't masturbating but making tea, about to sit down with some Raymond Carver stories. I didn't have to leap up from my futon and dress and return the pillow to its case and smooth the blanket. Turned out she'd locked herself out and needed a place to hang out awhile. I poured us tea and we sat on my futon. Doesn't this sound like a fantasy? A woman locks herself out of her apartment, knocks on your door, and asks to spend an indefinite amount of time with you in your apartment in which the only place to sit is your futon mattress. The girl's name was Frannie. She had dark hair and cocoa skin, like maybe she was Lebanese. The tip of her nose was flat. She had these soaked eyes with copper pupils and she wore a sweater that seemed not to cover but raise her pixie-like torso. The button to her jeans was undone, her silk turquoise panties smooching out. She was barefoot, her toes pebble-like. Had she stepped out to empty her trash in the trash and recycling room? She asked me all sorts of questions I can't recall. We could hear her roommate's footfalls on the hallway's industrial carpet followed by the creak of the door opening and then her flats clicking against the linoleum. Then a heavy bag dropping on a table and a few seconds later, water running and her talking on the phone. —You can hear everything, my neighbor said. —Yep, I said. —We never hear you at all, what's your problem? —I'm not here too much, which was a lie. I was there all the time. Frannie and I sat there looking at each other. My gaze dropped to her waist, that unfastened button folded back from olive skin like a marked page. Why didn't I make an advance? The situation seemed to be calling for it. Perhaps because I felt like such a loser yet maybe she wanted to be loser-fucked. That was, and still is all these years later, my problem, that gaping hole between how I think others perceive me and how others actually perceive me. I can't stop considering myself a loser, can't imagine why anybody would possibly want to be around me. The fantasy of my neighbor was more enjoyable than the possibility of something real during which I'd have to deal with my self-hatred and my proclivity to isolate myself. When an actual person expressed his or her desire to be with me, they perceived me as different than I perceived myself, which disoriented me, as if this person had me mistaken for somebody else and why would I want to be with a person who wanted to be with somebody else? Or it's as if a third person, the one desired, this me whom others seemed to enjoy, had entered the scene, making us an unhappy threesome, and this more familiar me, debased me, lonely me, inevitably forlorn, was now coming in between lover and beloved. The actual engagement itself—my neighbor and I sitting on my futon in my studio apartment, sipping tea, chatting—served as fodder for future masturbation sessions. More snapshots. The way she arched her back as she asked a question in her sugary impudent voice. The oblong patch of skin above the button unfastened. I enjoy your company but deep down I wish to walk away from you. I largely formed my sense of self in dreams. All the time I spent alone went towards those dreams. It didn't feel as if I was not doing much with my life but in actuality I was not doing much with my life. I had cultivated a very slow walk around the neighborhood. In the car I'd blast my Archers of Loaf cassette. I liked to imagine myself the lead singer and guitarist, playing a live show. I combined passionate musicianship with a smidge of ironic crowd detachment. Between songs I offered a thank you, yet my eyes remained on the set list taped to the stage next to the microphone stand. I didn't call a lot of attention to myself by engaging in stage antics. I wanted to project kindness and humility. Maybe at the end of the show, my body wringed out, I'd offer a sarcastic quip (—*We love you, Cleveland!*). I'd even pause the cassette tape so I could imagine, as I drove to work, the gestures I made as my band broke momentarily before beginning the next song. This rockstar thing had become for me a habitual escape from feeling like nobody in the world knew me. This feeling was false in that I didn't see how many people did know me. I'd identify a band I loved and whose music spoke to my implacable self-hatred (my father-anger) and become this band's lead guitarist, singer, and songwriter. Charlatans UK, Stone Roses, Superchunk, Archers of Loaf. I preferred an up and coming band from the Midwest, a male lead singer, e.g., Uncle Tupelo, Smashing Pumpkins. If I imagined myself, 23 years old, in a band like Sonic Youth or the Replacements, who'd been around for years, I'd think, this could not happen, Sonic Youth has been playing music since I was 12. There was very little chance I, as a 12-year-old boy living in Indiana, could have become singer and lead guitarist of an avant-garde punk band from New York City. By building a fantasy with more plausible elements I could more easily weld the fantastic to the actual. Of course this was plausible only in my dreamer's head, which sought out adoration without any of the sacrifice inherent in intimacy or expression, for I didn't play the guitar or sing, not even karaoke. Then again singing karaoke (real performance) didn't offer me the feeling of carrying around a secret in my heart. It's not that I lived my life only seeking out experiences to furnish my fantastic realms (I did), but I had no awareness my life with

my friends, my education, my passions for music and books, all
of this lay in elusive shadow of my waking dreams that were
fleshy and far-flung tendrils overcrowding my consciousness to
the extent I had to look through them to find the world external.
I carried these dreams with me as a small child totes with her
everywhere (to restaurants, on trips, to school) a stuffed animal,
though often stored away in dad's coat or mom's purse, not
visible, not intruding upon the instance (the silent accomplice,
the driver waiting in the running van) yet leave that child alone
and she breathes sensate life into that toy through which she
expresses her needs and fears and nascent desires, her disap-
pointments. My desire was the dream itself, that velvet-lined
cage, not padding me against the blow of reality but eclipsing it.
I didn't feel known by others, which made me angry at the world
and myself. I considered myself a fuck-up. Still do. To desire
to live alone is to desire to live among the people of my dreams,
those figments who know and love only the dream-me, but they
are not real like my wife and son are real and who know the
real-me, distracted me, sad and silly me, impatient and impulsive
me, me desperately looking for the next window of time in
which I can disappear. Walking through an alley that ran behind
student apartments and frat houses, sidestepping empty forty
ounce bottles and discarded plastic cups and endless piles of cigarette butts, on my way to a party at Strack or the Row Houses,
I was, in my mind, Jay Ponteri, lead singer for the Archers of Loaf,
a person who didn't boast or yap on about his band or equipment or road anecdotes (notice how my reticence served only to
enlarge my dream so that the real-me seemed to be vanishing),
and at the party, girls would tap their friend's shoulders, *There's
the singer for that band. Blah, blah ...* My fantasy band mates
were played by real friends, not close ones but newer friends for
whose attentions I yearned, friends who, from the distance of
newly acquainted, seemed to align with my own sense of self, the
self I wanted to be: disheveled to the point of destructive, sarcastic, well-read. My close friends didn't fit into my fantasy realm

only because I knew them as imperfect people full of contradictions that I was too self-absorbed to tolerate let alone appreciate.
Even though my band-mates-slash-friends and I didn't always
hang out or see each other in classes, we shared this bond, we
were in *that band*. During weekends we played local and regional
gigs and during breaks, Christmas and Summer, we headed out
on the road for club dates. After a party, drunk and stoned and
alone, without a girlfriend, I'd shut out the lights so I couldn't see
where I was, blast the Archers of Loaf through headphones,
standing in front of the mirror (the illusion of a witness?), lip
syncing, strumming an air guitar, imagining the show playing
out, one song to the next and at the end I'd smash my guitar like
Kurt Cobain although I couldn't imagine myself as Nirvana
because that would void out the existence of Kurt Cobain and
Kurt Cobain Existed (with a capital E), which is to say his hostile,
disheveled noise cut into me deeply, tearing through every layer
of my personality. Whatever girl on whom I had a crush played
bass or rhythm guitar. Like Sonic Youth's Kim and Thurston, we
were happy lovers off stage, we got each other, but on stage,
we were serious musicians, drawn to the notes we were playing,
to the beats inside. The rock journalists who interviewed us
commented about this, said, *You seem able to tune out adoring fans,
the slam dancers and bodies being passed in the air; it's like they're
not there* and the truth of the matter was they weren't. I find it
interesting that I wanted to be seen or known by others but only
dreamt up the distant, unsatisfying relationship between an
artist and her fans. My dreams had become an opaque mirror
through which I couldn't see my reflection. I imagined a film
actress (e.g., Winona Ryder or Parker Posey) jetting into Milwaukee, all this way to see me. An actual woman whom I hadn't the
courage to ask out or make advances on saw us, Winona and me,
Parker and me, at parties, standing next to the half-barrel,
filling up our cups. *I think the keg is almost done*, Winona-slash-
Parker said, her wrists, white and stick-like, punching out of her
sweater sleeves, and I said, smiling to the woman who sat next

to me in Chaucer, M W F, *Winona (Parker), here they say half-barrel
or quarter-barrel, not keg or pony keg*, and we snickered. I recall
one day, during winter, walking by Renee Row Apartments, headed
to my weed dealer's house on 19th and Kilbourn, the chilly air
seeping through my thin jacket, and film actress Julie Delpy (back
from Paris of course), said, *We need to buy you a winter coat*, and
I agreed, said, *Let's go shopping*, except I said this aloud, walking
by myself, not with Julie Delpy. A woman wearing a ski jacket
and wool muffler around her neck passing by asked, —Are you
talking to me? I can't say fantasy was an escape. For me it was
the place from which I began, where I defined for myself a sense
of self, my identity in relation to my surroundings. This sense of
self was different from the way my friends and family and pro-
fessors knew me and I couldn't reconcile these core differences
as various parts of a complex, mysterious personality – the dream-
me as brazen, adored, ubiquitous and the real-me as timid to
the point of peripheral, ever accommodating, a devout listener
and watcher, a shadow figure. I refused to tolerate this mystery I
couldn't grasp, thus came to despise this weaker part of me living
in the actual. Self-hatred grew out of self-confusion. In most
social situations with strangers I shrunk under my shyness and
self-hatred. This made me feel lonely. And night after night of
pouring pitchers of Pabst and whiskey shots for the same seven
or eight drunks made me feel even worse. Keying into my apartment and shutting the door, leaving the world behind, I'd feel an
enormous sense of possibility, a largeness in being. Once inside
I could retreat from the public spaces of work or school, of
community, teeming with people who at any moment could speak
at me or ask me to serve them. Inside I could save this self.
Inside I was well-liked and acclaimed. Brilliant. I imagined myself being interviewed by a fan of my writing or sitting on a panel
of writers and artists or hanging out backstage before a show. I
shared intimate moments with a woman I was too afraid to speak
to or to share my feelings with. As I walked around Farwell and
Locust streets, in and out of cafes and bookstores, I imagined

myself as a visiting writer, touring the retail district on my day off. The only thing I did that didn't seem to feed my dreams was shop for books. I was a ravenous bibliophile. Still am. Perhaps for me, walking through the literature or poetry sections of a bookstore is walking through my head, the way all those books revealed labyrinthine inner lives. Or the bookstore is like a book in which I so willingly lose myself. I searched for used hardcovered first editions of books I loved: *Ray* by Barry Hannah, *The Stories of Stephen Dixon. The Men's Club* by Leonard Michaels. I could not leave one bookstore unexplored. The last one I'd visit was Woodland Pattern, an airy, well-lit bookstore selling new books published by small presses. I imagined myself reading here to a gathering of students. In the Q and A, the awestruck audience asked me questions like, *How long did it take you to write this book? What's on your reading list these days? Is the novel's experience based on yours? Do you really masturbate with such theatrical flair?* But not questions like, *How do you balance songwriting with fiction writing? What does your band think of your fiction?* I couldn't mix these two fantasy realms because rarely, and I still believe this, do rockstars cross over and write decent prose and never do fiction writers or poets cross over and make interesting music. (Patti Smith is the exception!) Too many fantasy-accolades seemed unrealistic thus could only serve to remind me I was fantasizing, which I didn't want. At the time I didn't even like to admit to myself I lived inside my dreams, which had become my predominant way of being in the world to the point where I couldn't tease out the fantastic from the real. That pleasure of being swept up in not so much a narrative but in a thought stream both real and unreal. Often I wonder if I was padding myself. But against what? The uncertainty of young adulthood. My inability to reconcile the person I was with the person I was becoming. The disappointment of dailiness, of boredom, of accepting I'd have to fill so much of my time with activities that brought little or no meaning to my life. The shame I felt for no reason I could ascertain. The realization I wouldn't always or even often get what

I wanted. The feeling no matter what I did, I'd do it alone. Yet explaining away my propensity for dream, for this billowy life of the mind I lived, negates the pleasure of pushing into an imagined instance, the only place I seem to sustain a presence. My interior landscape feels expansive beyond reach, lush but not dense or humid. It has carved out a variety of topographies – from flat and prickly wintry fields to verdant backyard forests and gray blighted avenues on which one shouldn't walk alone but always does, dotted with buildings and houses and cafes and cathedrals whose rooms are lavishly arranged with couches and loungers and espresso carts complete with beautiful baristas holding my gaze next to entire walls of bookcases lined with my favorite books yet to be written or walls of windows looking out onto a placid shelf of slate sea or deep woods uncut with walking trails, rooms smartly lit with lemony light not too bright or too dim, illuminating nomadic paths to unseen nooks, capacious spaces of refuge, the best music (often the music of no-music) pumped through invisible speakers with mind-controlled volume, a ladder upwards into a barn loft carpeted with pillows, a door opening into a fond memory or a dream of adoration, the cottony prevalence of self-ness, a cranny or a closet where I raise the dress of a woman I cannot have, playing with strangers a game without end and there are no borders between exterior and interior, are one in the same, walking the field behind the Johnsons' house where us boys play baseball late into endless summer nights and in the outfield stands the door to the storage room where I hide the semen-stained pillow against which I masturbate, the storage room where I meet my mistress whose chest pours over mine like a drink for the drunk, all these spaces simultaneous and burgeoning, impossible to map, impossible to extract. On campus I'd entertain professorial fantasies. Walked into the English department and found my office down this very hall, behind this very door. Room 232. Sitting in my rickety oak chair, I puffed on a cigarette, looked out the window. A short break from grading essays or from meeting with students. A stroll around campus before my two p.m. lecture. Students hanging back afterwards for a casual chat before I sauntered back to my office. Or they visited during my posted office hours, seeking out guidance on matters personal and literary. Fingers entwined, legs crossed, head tilted, I was receptive, sincere, The Listener, giving their problems a dwelling place; my face, with its wide embrace and parted lips, saying, *Come to me.* This is a memory of a dream. Empty rooms of dust-sheeted furniture that go months, possibly years, without inhabitants. I'd eat lunch and then make my way to a café where I'd read my new book for a couple hours. I would be lying if I called it focused reading. I vacillated between the page with its rushing stream of words and the young women walking in the café. A few years younger than me, they were ensconced in the lethargic haze of attending classes, eating meals, studying, partying, maybe some part-time work as a waitress or a bartender, a job that merely enlivened one's social outlook. Kinky blond curls or long black bangs, cream white skin, light eyes darting. Back to the story with its obsessive, miserable char-acters until the bells tied to the café's glass door rang out and a new customer strolled in. I dreamt up elaborate fantasies, fictions, in which I and one of these women came together. She said, *Let me see your hand.* I held out my hand for her. My fingers trem-bled. She said, *Oh, I want to hold them, I want to hold them so they won't shake* and she did. She wrapped her hands around mine, her press-on nails like knife points against my wrist skin. *My main hobbies are smoking unfiltered cigarettes*, she said, *I occasionally like to snort a thick finger of cocaine.* She parted her terse lips as if to speak, then lifted her dress and took to the floor. I understood I would be the person to find her in bed, inebriated, overdosed, not breathing, a faint pulse. I would drive her to the emergency room and stay with her till she awoke and I'd be the person to tell her how lovely she was and how grateful I was that she was alive. In her diligent face, with its slivered lips and flashing eyes, I could see her anorexic mother and her somber, unpleasant father. I could see her yarn doll with its limp knit hands, could see

her needing her bottom lip to shield against all she couldn't control or understand and how she never went there save for dreams
of drowning.

AN ARTIST HOLDS an extended and steady gaze at the image
of his face he tries to make. This becomes ritual, a practice
beyond habit or need. Like swimming in the bottomless waters
of soul. He walks into his studio and confronts again the image
of his face he tries to make. Each new face, his face. His face. His
face. Tomorrow, again. Next week, his face. Consider a man
who sins, then prays for forgiveness. He does this every day, sins,
then prays – through repetition brought closer to god.

I RECALL SUNDAY pasta mom made from scratch on Saturday,
the pasta drying overnight on sheets of waxed paper, the house
filling with the simmering sauce, the sausage, garlic, onion, basil,
tomato. Us boys left the house with that aroma sticking to our
skin. Back inside we'd ask, —How long? And mom would say,
—A while. Like traditional Italians, mom and dad used forks to
twirl pasta into neat bunches that were then dropped on soup
spoons. The oldest one sucked-smacked one strand at a time. To
get me to laugh with a mouthful of milk, the middle one lifted
his hand to his mouth-and-nose holes and fake-sneezed and then
opened his hand to nibbled meatball. —How long? —A while.
How I ate my pasta, I don't recall, the watcher I was, still am watching this family eat even after we've stopped eating together,
never will the five of us eat together again. Afterwards we lament
wearing white instead of red. Pointing at the splotch of spilled
sauce on our shirts, we say, —Look, the map of Italy!

MOM NOTICED THE dog wheezing, noticed short breaths,
noticed hard kibble in the dog's bowl at day's end and the dog
curled into herself on the couch. No rushing into kitchen at the
sound of kibble ting-ing the ceramic, no gobbling, no licking
the bowl clean, the dog, our sweet kitchen helper, as we called her.

Listening to the dog's stilted heartbeat, the vet frowned at my
mom, his eyes watery and his lips crooked, fluttering, an insect
whose wings were pinned to a board, saying to mom, —It's
getting close, you should make the decision sooner than later.
Our vet spoke in a caring, pestered tone of voice, as if he were
gently shaking mom's shoulders or flicking drops of cold water in
her dazed face. Just that morning the dog had eaten her kibble,
mom explained to our vet, the dog stood at the sliding glass door
to be let outside and mom laid the dog down amidst myrtle and
hyacinth, the autumn's weak, white sunlight nuzzling its black
coat. Mom didn't mention blood traces she'd found in the dog's
stool or the dog's whimpering, reminding her of the glow from a
night light in a child's bedroom, that safe guide, that top blanket,
the truth being mom wanted me, her youngest son, the one who
seemed to stay with her the longest, longer than her husband
although the dog stayed like nobody else had, the dog trailing her
from kitchen to TV room to basement (laundry) and back to
bedroom, its wagging tail thudding walls, glass coffee table, chairs.
Mom wanted me to say goodbye to the dog before the dog drew
its last breath on earth then no more. Mom wanted to have the dog
and her youngest one together one last time. Mom scratched
behind the dog's ears or rested her head gently against the dog's
muzzle, saying, —Just hang on. The youngest one's coming
home soon. You remember the youngest one, you remember how
you used to keep him from leaving the house for school. You
wanted him to stay home and play ball with you, take you for
meandering walks through the woods or on snowy days when the
township canceled school, the two of you would cut through
back woods and the youngest one would raise his head to glimpse
cream-colored sky through spindly branches snow-covered, the
whorl of flakes dropping while you ran what looked to me from
the second floor window from which I watched figure-eights
around the maples and willows and when you didn't want him to
leave the house, you'd hide his winter cap in your basket of chew
toys. If he found it, you'd knock him down and strip the hat off

his head. That's when you were a puppy and the youngest one
was still a boy and you had all kinds of energy. —Hold on, mom
whispered, lips pressed to the dog's ear, ear flap back-folded,
—Let the youngest one come home to say goodbye. Mom held off
on putting the dog to sleep till mid-September when, back from
Prague, I drove the toll road through Gary, Indiana, past the
great towers of stacks spewing inky-black smoke into a slate sky,
towards my hometown no longer my hometown. I carried the
dog outside to the little patch of grass in the front yard and we sat
there as the brisk breeze tossed leaves curled under. Scratching behind the dog's ears and underneath her muzzle, I recalled
how the dog as a puppy (no longer a puppy) had knocked my
tiny body over and lapped my face with wet kisses and then
galloped off into the woods surrounding our house no longer a
house. At night I hand-fed her one piece of kibble at a time, wiped
crud from her eye. I brought the dog back to mom's bedroom and
the next morning I left for Milwaukee to begin my post-college
life, a writer's life, while my mom, unbeknownst to me, took the
dog to the vet and put her to sleep. Mom phoned afterwards.
I said, —I could've gone with you, I could've been there, and mom
said, her voice sorry and scraped, —I needed to do it. Another
way of saying, *Everybody left the house with the dog and me left
inside*. Or *the dog shared her whole life with me*, which is not the
saddest part of the story, the saddest part for me is the vet shaving
a patch of skin on the dog's foreleg, the needle pinching her skin,
then puncturing the vein, the overdose of anesthesia entering
her bloodstream and the dog's whole body trembling as mom
holds on to the dog's haunches.

Before Video Games

IN THE MIDDLE AGES, UNIVERSITY BOYS PLAYED A GAME called shinnies. With jagged rocks clenched in fists, two boys took turns hitting each other as hard as they could in the shins. Last boy standing won. Twenty-pound rats scurried across stone floors as other boys – all armed with knives, hammers, or bludgeons – watched till it was time to head off to the next lecture on astronomy or rhetoric or law, leaving behind the loser lying in a bowl of his own blood.

The Manuscript (V)

IN BED MY WIFE ASKED ME ABOUT THE MANUSCRIPT. I wrote 90 minutes a day, five days a week, all this time spent exploring our marriage separate from my wife. I understood why she was curious and I understood why she rarely asked me about it. Inside our refrigerator within the crisper drawer tightly shut, a lettuce head rotted. Walking past, you couldn't smell a thing. I said to my wife, —I'm trying to figure out why people marry. Do people who marry know why they marry? I mean, I knew you wanted to get married and I wanted to be with you and all of your friends at that time were marrying, my brothers too. I recall thinking that I would marry at some point. I never questioned it. I asked my wife, —Don't you think people should hold particular relationship talents before marrying? At least make engaged couples answer a questionnaire. Just because I share feelings of love with another person doesn't mean I know how to navigate a relationship with her, doesn't mean I know how to love or be loved. My hunger signals the need to eat, to reach out for food yet doesn't tell me what or how to maintain a healthy diet. I'm discerning between a feeling and its emanation, between, as Anne Carson deftly argues in *Eros The Bittersweet*, desire's reach and subsequent possession. We don't know how to possess because possession is an illusion, that is, it's impossible to truly possess anything for longer than a moment and even in that moment (as I chewed a bite of sweet-potato fry or as I drove her to the airport or slid aside the damp crotch of her panties),

am I really possessing her or is she merely passing through my
hands? Impermanence. We never arrive, we're in continuous
transit or we do arrive but only at death. Fucking can be construed
as a means to possession but even the ecstatic pleasure that
often (but not always) accompanies fucking disappears once the
fucking is done. Not even through memory can we hold something. I was on a rant here, paying no attention to my wife's feet
warm against mine or her hand holding my arm or the dried
flowers once pinned to her wedding dress now hanging over the
bedpost or the clenched fist of her shut eyes, the lids tight and
wrinkled like waxed paper. —I mean, romantic love is fleeting and
marriage isn't forever. People change. They become other
people they hadn't planned on becoming when they first came
together. Who could've predicted I'd never want to leave the house
or not answer the telephone? Jesus, look at our parents. What
if you grow into people who share nothing but time passed and
here's another moment we've shared but not really shared
because we both feel lonely and the fica tree behind the rocking
chair moves into shadow. —What remains? I asked my wife.
—Neck pains from always turning around to look back, I said to
my wife. —Where has my passion gone? I have to grope like a
16-year-old for a memory of my desire for you and I know you hate
that word, *horny*, I said. She said, —I do hate that word, the way
it mingles sexual excitement and goat anatomy. —We're pretty
much goats. Or goat-like. —I'd say we're more evolved than goats.
—Take my parents, I said, —Eighteen years after they divorce
mom said dad seems like a distant cousin she never sees. A week
later mom said she's still miffed dad canceled a hot-air-balloon
ride in 1982. I mean, attachment and love are like rat and mouse.
You'd think they get along fine but one eats the other. —What
an enormous generalization, my wife interrupted. —You act like
every relationship is doomed.

MY WIFE AND I came together during a period of my life in
which I was not myself. Instead of considering what I wanted, I

looked to my older brothers for guidance. They were grown-up, bill-paying folk. Newlyweds. The real-me was a leaking, meddling voice I tried to hush. That voice said things like, —Relax, read a novel or a book of poems. Time for a cigarette. Smoke a joint? Smoke another joint? —What's wrong with getting paid under the table? I asked. I guess you could say this real-me differed vastly from the perceptions I held of my brothers. Unlike them I couldn't hold it together. Bills and parking tickets piled up unpaid and I stopped answering the telephone, for the caller only wanted to punish me. There were the bartending jobs and my refusal to cut my hair or type up a resume. Instead of searching for a job, I stayed in my studio apartment and read *Crime and Punishment* and listened to Nirvana and wrote bad stories about characters who behaved poorly in ways that didn't reflect my life. The characters in those early stories set fire to ratty couches at house parties and got laid a lot whereas I was a loner, too afraid to damage other people's property or ask a woman if she'd like to come with me to my apartment. My behavior was that of a meek depressive. Aside from reading books and writing and women, I held no other interests. I take that back–I played a lot of pinball at a bar called Conway's. I guess I mentioned the part about smoking a lot of weed. Oh, I also enjoyed hanging out with friends and by *friends* I mean any lost, irreverent soul willing to talk shit into the early morning hours in some stranger's kitchen or over a greasy breakfast at George Webb's or at the lakefront waiting for the sun to rise. I refused to go to bed out of some mysterious need to stop the next day. The next day I had to work or not work or decide what to do with my life and my bank account balance would dip into the negative. The next day I could die. I didn't die. I'd wake up around three in the afternoon to weak winter light and a cold in my nose. I'd get dressed, stumble through dirty snow to the convenience store for burnt coffee and cigarettes. I'm pretty sure my car got towed at some point. This real-me confounded my family or that's what I thought. The truth is they were living their own lives, albeit very different ones from mine,

but they had their own loads to shoulder and so perhaps they
didn't know anything about this real-me. I believed I was the problem. I should be more like them or perhaps I thought I could
be more like them. I considered getting back together with an ex-
girlfriend from high school. This ex- was silly and fun yet able
to compose herself around others too (the word *elegant* comes to
mind, also the word *caring*) and she was beautiful and I knew
my family liked her, liked the fact her dad was a medical doctor.
She was marriage material, or that's what I thought at the time.
(One often uses this phrase *marriage material* to describe another's
potential to live within marriage. Seldom do we use the phrase
in self-appraisal. That is to say, before we consider our own capacity to live inside of a relationship, we pick apart another person's
behavior, appearance, class, and speech. And we judge. Any
semblance of social anxiety or awkwardness, extreme reticence,
mental instability, or sustained poverty can limit or even exclude
another from being described as marriage material. The focus
has veered from valid feelings of an uncertain self towards my dim
perceptions of what others find acceptable or normal. By thinking the thought, *my ex- was marriage material*, I was turning away
from my feelings.) This ex-girlfriend was nothing like the woman
I presently dated – she was a real match flicker, a raised middle
finger, definitely *marriage immaterial* or *marriage ethereal*. The
night she met dad and his new wife, this present girlfriend wore
a close-fitting silver T-shirt over a short silver skirt, silver plat-
form shoes, silver eye shadow, and sparkly silver lipstick. My step-
brother later reported to me he thought I'd picked her up in
outer space. Around our dinner table, she said the word *fucking*
at least 10 times. As an adjective. As in, *Those fucking clowns
always play craps on the sidewalk outside my house*, or *Do you mind
if I step outside on the patio, I'm fucking jonesing for a cig here*. At
one point dad asked her what her father did – this a question dad
often asked of my friends – and she said he built log cabins. I wish
I could recall what dad's face looked like at that moment.
The slight folds in his brow might have belied the feigned delight

expressed by his moist eyes and upturned mouth. I know it sounds like I'm picking on dad here but work was (and is) the lens through which dad looks out at the world and he had some particular ideas about what a man should do for a living or at the least what kind of ambitions a man should have and building log cabins did not make the list. Neither did writer. In all honesty my present girlfriend was better suited to the real-me than was my ex. Which is to say, my present girlfriend and I both felt some part of ourselves had died and everywhere we went we carried around that death. A favorite activity of ours was to snort anything we could fit into our nasal cavities – cocaine, Ritalin, speed, aspirin. In the bedroom, she liked to handcuff me to the broken radiator and then sit on my face or she'd say, her voice lacing concupiscence with a schoolgirl's hesitance, —How would you like to suck my twatty-twat? Even though her roommate was in the next room playing Sega, she'd scream louder than I'd ever imagined a woman screaming during sex. I thought I should try to pull myself together. I cannot stop my love for dad or my need for his approval. It's hard to flip him off again and again. Pay my bills on time. Be a man. Forgive dad for hurting mom by walking out on their marriage and for hurting me by mistaking me for a man who wore khaki pants and shirts with collars and enjoyed stock talk. That was around the time I broke things off with the screamer and called my ex-girlfriend. I admit our desire for each other was substantial but ours was a thin love, an it's-a-good-idea-on-paper love, the long-distance love between lovers inhabiting the same bed. Although I should not reduce the great need I had at that time for connectivity, to touch and be touched by a like and different creature, to form a picture of myself with another that might supplant the picture of me alone and broken. Perhaps, at that time, I reached for her exactly because she didn't fit, that humans do not fit together despite the fact we need to reach out to one another, that our inevitable marriage demanded I take (as one says) *a leap of faith* in what was and is essentially mysterious and impossible, and to this day, sadly, I have not leapt, have no faith in mystery, in my wife's capacity to surprise me, in her beauty and compassion. Our eye contact is not so good these days. We came together, our desire faded, we got engaged. Ahhh, the last boy was getting married. I felt lonely in my heart but thought such feelings were wrong. Those feelings squeaked with every step I took and my response was not to wear a different pair of shoes or at the least investigate from where the squeak came but to feign deafness. I acted on what I believed others expected. What others thought and did made perfect sense. Get married. Now, years later nothing makes sense to me. It doesn't make sense to me that mine and my wife's separate feelings of loneliness, the particular sadness of our marriage, has given rise to a new variety of love – not passionate love or sweet love or pity love but a dogged love, a love whipped and wounded and blown through, the love of estranged siblings who don't think to call each other but on a last-minute road trip to a funeral of a distant cousin, they don't mind splitting a single room at the Super 8 or sharing a queen-sized bed. Their backs or knees accidentally touch in the night and that's OK or if it's not OK, neither one speaks up. Mother has been dead for a long time.

AT THE END of *The Graduate*, in what one might call the film's denouement, that is, *after* Benjamin steals Elaine away from her wedding, they run away from the church. They board what appears to be a city or regional bus, out of breath, giddy, and make their way *down the aisle* towards the empty seats at the back of the bus, and meanwhile other riders are gawking at them, at the spectacle they are making of themselves, Elaine in a rumpled wedding dress and Benjamin in worn street clothes, their faces flushed with sweat and color, their wide grins full of blissful incredulity. They laugh in amazement at what they've just done. As the bus pulls away, their faces slacken. They look away from each other. Perhaps the reality of what they have done dawns on them. They have broken up Elaine's wedding and her future life with The Make-Out King (*He said we'd make a good team*), and they have potentially severed ties to their respective families of origin, to Benjamin's parents, to the Robinsons who are divorcing. Benjamin and Elaine are together *and* alone in the world. This seems a slightly exaggerated but nuanced representation of marriage, that is, when we marry, we close ourselves off to the world. What happens inside of marriage remains unseen. A marriage's daily mechanics, its habits and rituals, its meaning-ful and deleterious expressions, its omissions, its caverns, its rooftop views, how it reaches up to the light and lies in dreamy shadow at night, all remains hidden from view and what others do see is an illusion of a surface (a not-surface) made of their own distorted projections of what their marriage should or shouldn't be. I cannot touch my own beating heart. *We are not so good at this*. Back on the bus, Elaine blows a hair from her eye, begins to think about her mother, Mrs. Robinson, not how sad and broken-down and desperate she is or how hateful she has become but how Elaine doesn't know her mother. Feeling the sting of her cheek from her mother's open hand, Elaine wonders about her mother's wedding day. Was her mother happy? Did her mother want to run away from her father? Benjamin's thoughts also return to Mrs. Robinson, to her naked body under stiffly starched hotel sheets, how in the pitch-dark of the room 568 in the Taft Hotel they made love without saying a single word to each other. What will we do with our lives? Where is this bus taking us?

IN BED MY wife said to me how funny it was that married couples slept in the same bed, how we spent the entire day doing things separately or together, jobs, telephone calls, hobbies, dinner, laundry, mulch in the yard, you did the bath and I read the story, you read and I watched TV and then, without question, we convened in the same bed and usually not to have sex. We came to rest together, to fall asleep, to dream, to replenish our energy for the day following. Sometimes we held each other but mostly we read or talked or my wife wrote in her journal or we watched a show on our laptop but not anything we couldn't easily do with

a friend or a sibling or even our parents, lie in bed next to each
other before turning in separate directions, off to sleep. We
shared a bed. Perhaps, if we didn't share a bed, we would also not
share the potential for sexual intimacy, one kind of adhesive for
not all marriages but many, that is to say, if we cut each other off
from that possibility, we would be no different than friends or
siblings, Lucy and Ricky, Fred and Ethel, close but not too close,
rather separate from each other yet therein lay part of our
problem, that during the day I felt so separate from my wife, that
outside of bed we did not move like lovers moved, we did not
touch each other or I did not touch my wife, sensually or sexually,
that is, me touching the back of her neck or taking her hand or
embracing her or kissing her or her cuffing my crotch or guiding
my finger to brush hers and outside of bed it was easier to
distract ourselves, to draw our attention from the loneliness of
our bodies, check e-mail or iron or throw in another load of
laundry, distract ourselves from the illusion – that our playing
house was enough to sustain a marriage – that seemed to hold us
together, like a bed could hold any two bodies, exhausted bodies
in need of replenishment, of repose. In bed it was more difficult
to ignore the reality beneath this illusion (our separateness), and
to ignore the fact that this illusion was, to paraphrase Paul
Auster's translation of Frenchie Joseph Joubert, *an emanation, an
effluvia in disappearance*. Perhaps sharing the bed was our last
hope for intimacy, also not much of a hope because not engaging
in any intimacy during the day made it difficult to feel close at
night, or being together where we couldn't be distracted by doing
email or cleaning the kitchen or our son or the pile of mulch
or the neighborhood newsletter only more clearly revealed our
separateness, i.e., our bed was our marriage. Our bed was our
lack of hope, the space in which we couldn't deny our separateness. Her reach for me was met by resistance or my wanting to
fuck her met by her pain over my desire for Frannie, by her knowledge I wanted to fuck somebody else, I wanted to love somebody
else. Even though our bed framed a possibility for intimacy, say

after we had spent some time talking about the nature of our mutual feelings of separateness, or after we yelled and wept and felt the heaviness of our complicated marriage and we wanted to soothe each other, wanted to lick each other's wounds and we'd fuck not so much out of desire but out of sorrow and remorse, out of a desire to be something we were not, to be something other than we were, that kind of sorrowful intimacy, our bed was the place we confronted the void of our intimacy. Our marriage was dying, it was sick and we didn't know how to care for it, didn't understand what made it sick, were afraid to admit we needed somebody to care for us and then I was getting tired and lonely – self-destruct button set – about ready to kill it, put our intimacy out of its misery as we lay next to each other, not even able to share the sorrow of our loss.

JAPANESE ARTIST NOBUYOSHI Araki considers his photography as a diary, each image recording a swollen moment in his life. His photographs not only record memory but replace it. As his young wife, dying of cancer, neared the end of her life, already having slipped into unconsciousness, he squeezed her hand and hers clenched his and realizing this might be the last time his wife responded to the touch of any human being, he asked his brother, in the hospital room with them, to pick up his camera and from a rather oblique angle, shoot a photograph of their hands touching. Araki says, —One part of me watches what's going on and another part snivels. Even at a time like that.

IN BED WITH my wife: —Don't you think people marry for reasons that are at best mysterious and at worst totally misguided? *My friends are married, my brothers and sisters married, I want a wedding.* It's like that dumb kid's song. *First comes love, then comes marriage, then comes baby in a baby carriage.* —Come on, my wife said, which really meant *Get your head out of your ass.* My wife sat up. She wore one of my T-shirts, way too large for her but comfortable for turning over in the night, and plain underpants

nipped with holes. No close fitting tank top, no slim panties rasp-
berry-colored with toenails painted to match. I imagined my
wife saying, Every guy fantasizes women sitting around in bra and
panties. A fucking panty party. But, I imagine myself saying
to my wife, Are there women who actually do some menial tasks
around the house in bra and panties? Don't some (not all)
women become the things we men dream up? I began to feel cold
without my wife's feet warming my leg. For the record I did not,
I repeat, I did not fantasize Frannie in panties traipsing around
her apartment with dust feather in one hand, cigarette in other.
Not a bad picture, though. My wife said, —Are you saying we
shouldn't have married? Her lips twitched. —No, I said, —Not at
all, I said. I said, —I'm saying there's a mysterious force at work,
a force that gives rise to a need for marriage and when I say the
word *force* I'm not speaking about religion. More of a biological
force, some chemical mix in the brain. Perhaps this force is *the
mystery of personality* (as Flannery O'Connor called it). The way
we know and don't know each other. The way our lives turn
towards mystery. Like we have to know things we don't know and
go to great lengths to do so. Even though we know (or do not
know) that we will never know. In the dark, looking at the coat tree
but thinking I see a person hunched over against the wall. Those
white underpants with pebble-sized holes, one or two in the
crotch, others bespeckling the elastic around hip and hip, those
white underpants with stretched elastic, those white underpants I launder every week, each pair faintly stained with blood
or sweat or semen. I sort them in with other lights – e.g., sheets,
athletic socks, towels, cloth napkins, rags with which she cleans
her paint brushes. Once they've been washed and dried, I fold
each pair in a triangle, stack them in a pile, really more of a tower,
a leaning tower of my wife's plain white underpants. Bless my
wife, bless her white underpants. Bless me, bless my boxer shorts
of rubbed, tattered cotton. Bless their fading colors, bless our
ugly ordinariness.

I BEGAN TO feel like a creep. I told myself to cease all contact with Frannie. Stop expressing my desire for her to her. Let her go. Let me feel the loss of her. Touching the bloody tear where I ended and her non-presence began, I filled with desire for her, that is, confronting my loss became another way of being carried away by my desire for her and this made me want to contact her, I found any excuse to email or telephone her, I opened a blank email or text message, giving rise to the feeling I was a creep, that is, and I couldn't have articulated this at the time, my desire for her (expressed to her) hurt her, my desire obliterated any sense of self-recognition, hers or mine.

A KNOCK AT the door.

    Do I answer?

    No.

    Why not?

    Because I cannot face the person knocking at the door.

    The person knocking at the door wants something from me and I'd prefer to remain inside.

    Inside the house?

    Inside my thoughts.

I CONTINUE TO speak to you in my thoughts. I continue to speak to a woman who does not hear me. I speak to only those who cannot hear me.

BITING A BITTEN-DOWN fingernail, my wife said, —I get what you're saying. i.e., we are drawn to what we don't know and even after we think we know, we remain mysterious to each other. I get that. We have to keep digging with a shovel even after the shovelhead begins to rust. But the plain truth is I'm not uncertain in the way you are. I can't imagine being with another man. I don't look at a man on the street and imagine myself pulling down his boxer shorts. I'm not prone to such fantasy. (Typing away at the mall's food court, I ogle a college-aged woman – face, hair, chest, hips, ass, calves. I imagine bark-red pubic hair.) My reply, secretly that was, not to my wife's face, was that I didn't believe my wife. Did she not look at another man and imagine his calloused fingertips, say, a carpenter's fingertips, a man who worked with his hands, these hands touching her cheeks? Did she not yearn for new thighs underneath her buttocks? Did she not dream of a man with a flatter tummy and thicker eyebrows? A man who made her laugh more than I did. A man who hiked and camped. A man who didn't need to be at the airport three hours before departure time. A man whose inner life included her. A man who's not so lost inside. —How are you uncertain? I asked, —You said you were not uncertain in the way I was. —I'm uncertain, my wife said, —Because you're uncertain. I never know what's going on in your head. I don't want to be angry with you but when we're having sex I want to box you. For all I know in your head you'd rather be fucking some other woman. Like Frannie. This name, Frannie, sputtered from my wife's lips, the first time she said Frannie's name aloud to me. (We cannot be saved from our ordinariness.) —I want to reiterate, I said to my wife, —That some of my fantasies, or dreams, let's call them dreams. —You say dreams, I say fantasies, my wife said. —The dreams enacted in my manuscript originate from a deep loneliness that's tied to the identity issue, you know, me not feeling known by you. My wife said, —I've been working on that, which was true enough. She'd stopped inviting strange people to our house on the weekends (my parents in the 1980s called such people, company, which to me suggested work) and she'd started buying me cigarettes, as if to say, I'll help you kill you, and the other day she'd even asked me to recommend a novel for her to read. —Even if I'm willing to recognize this sadder self and I am, always have been, are you going to share this part of yourself with me or are you going to save it for some manuscript you won't let me read or for some strange woman who has no idea you rarely brush your teeth before bedtime? —I floss. —When do you share this sadder self with me? —Right now, I said, —We're talking, are we not?

—What aren't you telling me? —There's nothing I'm not telling you, I lied.

I'M NOT COMFORTABLE with my wife holding me, staring at me, expressing she is there with me for me. When I feel her attention, I turn away. What might happen if I stay with my wife? If I stay with her staying with me. If I stay with her staying with me wanting to be elsewhere. Not elsewhere *and* not with my wife holding me. To not be in two places at once. Beyond nowhere.

I BEGAN TO scratch my wife's back, my fingernails crisscrossing her skin. After like five minutes I tickled her thigh, snaked index and middle fingers (little feelers) towards her groin but the moment they so much as skimmed across the cottony field of her white underpants she recoiled and what I mean by recoiled is her legs buckled to her chest, not just assuming the fetal position but clutching to it, as if things were not OK and she needed the protection of her mother's womb or she needed to protect her baby. Impatient and indignant I sat up in bed. I sighed. Our dogs snored. The sheets were stiff and dry after being laundered with her white underpants. I scrunched the top sheet in my fist and maybe at the same time or a second later I gnashed my teeth. Fist, then teeth. Or fist and teeth. Usually I gnashed my teeth without realizing I was doing so. Relax your jaw, I'd tell myself. My wife said to me, —You know I'm sick of carrying around this anger. Maybe pain is a better word. I really am. If I knew how, I'd make it disappear. I would. Blips of pasty moonlight slipped through the window and curtains onto the duvet. The light fixture seemed to hover beneath the ceiling. Didn't every marriage hold a certain amount of despair? Could we shoulder that despair together and could we continue walking to the same destination even if I wasn't comfortable holding hands? What was our destination? Death? What held us together aside from our despair and our sleeping son? Why was I so afraid to live alone? What happened when what held you together was toxic? What happened when one held the other holding nothing but himself? What happened when two people couldn't identify what held them together or they could, but identified different, oppositional things? What happened when my wife's love for me depended on marriage whereas mine for her largely involved her mothering our child? How did lovers fall from love? Like this. My wife asked, —Have you ever tried so hard but failed to get rid of something inside of you? —I have, I said, but didn't say what or how. Didn't embrace my wife who sniffled so faintly so that her nasal upsuck sounded like somebody crumpling a dead leaf in her fist. Didn't say fist and teeth. Didn't say I tried to stop obsessing over Frannie. Like I'd give myself limits on how often I could check my email per day and that number fluctuated according to how easily I could fool myself into thinking I was not betraying my wife. Or I'd focus on Frannie's flaws. She was a depressive, a compulsive shopper, dreamily self-absorbed, shy, a pack-a-day smoker and a recovering addict, although, save for the fact that I'd never battled alcohol addiction, though God forbid I gave up my cigarettes or my habit of smoking a joint on Friday nights, Frannie and I shared flaws, yes, we did, which was the 47th way to say, *Frannie, I love you.* I said to my wife, —I don't know how you let things go. My guess is time passes and you outlast it. Or you don't. Scar tissue forms, you carry it with you the rest of your life. —I want to let it go, my wife said. —But maybe you can't, maybe the damage is permanent till you die, I said. —Let's just have sex. And no clit play, I'm not in the mood. Just fuck and lie. Not out of pleasure or desire for me but to satisfy my need. The opposite of erotic. Mechanical, without feeling, worse than masturbation in that way. In my mind's eye, Frannie materialized, ribbons of tangled brassy hair, mouth ajar, full lips spit-laden. I didn't want to see Frannie. I did. My problem is I can lie to my wife's face but not when I write. There was always a Frannie in my life, a Frannie inside of me keeping me from my wife and son, or should I say, I was keeping myself from my wife and son? My wife was not exactly enjoying herself. Her eyes were squinted and her jaw and chin were pulled taut like a flexed muscle. My concentration lapsed. It ended up taking me awhile. After I finally came inside my wife, instead of beelining it to the bathroom to towel off, I stayed in bed in the dark with my wife. Swiping tears from her cheeks and wiping her dripping nose with her finger, she said, —You know it's my fault it takes you so long. From childbirth. It's different. —No, I said, —It's my fault. I did this to you. I pulled her closer to me. I felt love for her in this moment: she was broken and I'd broken her. I was slasher and suturer, the author of this instance and I knew it would appear in my manuscript, though not exactly as it occurred, for I'm prone to fabricate speech or exaggerate a gesture and of course memory is an act of the imagination and once the manuscript was done and parts or all of it were published or not published, I knew my wife would have to read it and I knew her reading it could destroy our marriage, that is, she would have to decide upon seeing my inner life revealed in these pages whether or not she could cope with the rejection she'd feel and I would understand if she needed to leave me. I recall something Leonard Michaels said about Raymond Carver, how Carver had fully mined his first marriage to Maryann Carver to write his early stories or that he'd given over his first marriage to the writing of those early stories or that he'd sacrificed his marriage for the making of those early stories. Something like that – I can't recall exactly what. I do recall what a friend of mine, a poet, said about the speaker of this very essay after reading an earlier draft, that it felt to him like the speaker was about to cheat on his wife. It's not that I felt caught or guilty, as if he were uncovering something I knew but others didn't, but I do remember feeling stunned in the way one feels upon seeing before him, for the first time, his inevitable future.

I WILL NOT demonize adultery as a shameful, reprehensible act. I do not see it as a deviation or as a failure. Adultery is commonplace behavior. Even if you have not engaged in an adulterous relationship or have not been hurt by the betrayal of your spouse or partner, you might have been tempted by the other (fantasy-fucked your boss or your friend's husband or your contractor), or perhaps you are excessively fascinated by adultery in TV or film, or maybe you feel a physical repulsion towards adulterers, or you have (as we all have) gossiped about a friend's, family member's, or co-worker's affairs, or perhaps you have been fortunate enough to read about, consider, and discuss adultery with a supportive, thoughtful community, say, at church or school or with your therapist or a men's group or book club. We do not live in isolation but in communities. Our lives, our habitual and non-habitual actions, link in inextricable, unfathomable ways. We mimic and model, we behave in concert with one another, we choose otherwise, in spite of, we rebel, we revolt. We do bad things because we can (Dostoyevsky). I throw, you catch. You drop it, are too bored to pick it up. One person's choices create and exclude possibilities for others. We are all complicit here, for our bodies are in fast decay, and whether we admit it or not, we remain uncertain about our feelings, and our identities are in flux. To shame the act of adultery is to pretend we are strange to one another and thus *to remain* strangers to one another. Shame separates us from any awareness around not only the adulterous act but the context out of which it arises – love and marriage. Unfortunately there is a tight, toxic silence around marriage and its (dis)contents. We may talk inside of marriage (intra), but rarely do we, as couples or on our own, talk across or outside of our marriages, save for gossip of friends and family, which is interesting but also indirect, even a form of masking one's own fears and struggles. Perhaps our resistance to this inter-relationship talk stems from marriage's proprietary nature. We want to protect our spouses and the intimacy we share (or do not share, or struggle to share) but protect from what? From judgment? From scrutiny? From loneliness? From the difficulty of facing the fact that things end, that we die alone, that we leave others behind, that we want to leave others behind? This desire to protect, which itself is unacknowledged (thus unspoken), seems only to excuse our silence rather than offer insight into why and when and how we cease expression. I believe this silence largely stems from our fears of failure and our fears to confront these failures – not only our personal failures at marriage but our culture's collective failure at marriage, the failure of an institution. How difficult it is to acknowledge we have entered into such a flawed, fragile dwelling. How difficult it is to talk about what we cannot so easily name or what we may not be very good at or what may seem hurtful to others. What is love supposed to look like and feel like? What comprises love? How do we deepen our love for each other? What if our love disappears? John Armstrong defines love *as the secret self finding a home in the eyes of another.* John Armstrong says love is *governed by unconscious forces causing us to attach ourselves to somebody with whom we can repeat a self-harming pleasure.* Perhaps the qualities that comprise (or arise from) love – e.g., desire, passion, generosity, envy, anger, destruction even – do not strengthen a marriage but burn it out. The phrase "starter marriage" is a start at a conversation yet to happen. The American poet (not the British singer) Chris Martin asks *how can we speak in the common language that binds us of the things that that bond obliterates?* To write close to my private life, to speak openly about my feelings and to do so uncloaked, as an essayist, as one who attempts (but fails with dignity) to understand is to tear through the fabric of this very real silence. Often the adulterous act is a characteristic (rather than a symptom) of a larger identity recalibration, enacting a person's complicated desire to be known differently than he or she feels known inside of his or her marriage. And (or) it is the next rung on a short or long ladder to the destruction of self, of others. (Because we can.) Established, practiced roles in a monogamous relationship might diminish our capacities to feel desire, love, and empathy for each other. What we desire is borne out of strangeness, but our comfort with habit and order lead us away from the stranger possibilities. Choosing one partner and that person's unique characteristics closes off the possibility of loving another person with uniquely

different characteristics. I will say that again. James Richardson
says real love includes the desire to forgive. Toni Nelson says
love is sadness. Scott Nadelson says sometimes a relationship
just runs its course. Marrieds are marrieds, not lovers but
fuckers, or non-fuckers, yet we certainly would not guess that by
watching Hollywood-made movies or television. Marriage
seems to increase loneliness not mitigate it. I mean, perhaps two
cheaters fall in real, deep love with each other. You are the fuck-
love of my life. The healthiest of relationships endure myriad
separations and reconciliations. We fall in and out of love. Marriage cushions, does not cushion its lovers. I want to discuss
all of this with you. What do you think? Please tell me. Our shame
only breeds silence, denial, and illusion. (*He does not say it but
I know he loves me.*) This manuscript is a dream, my dream of a
discussion, which is to say, it is different from any dream you
might have or make. It is also a dream of my sorrow, my desire.
The prose does not censor itself. Making art forces one to practice
a kind of divergent thinking in which one considers many
answers to a single question, many solutions to a single problem.
This manuscript cannot be fact checked. Recall is slippery, an
act of the imagination, a manifestation of desire. I made some
stuff up. Its contents might upset you or hurt you. You might react
on my wife's behalf. You might imagine (feel) the pain of my
betrayal and of my rejection of her and as a result become angry
with me. This only makes sense, for our love over time for one
another affords us the capacity to feel one another's pain. I do not
apologize. I can hold your frustration. You can write me or speak
to me. Leonard Michaels says (in *Journal*), *One of Byron's letters
was made into a poem. Real intimacy is for the world, not a friend.* I
wrote this book as if nobody in the world would ever read it and
here I am, wanting it to be read by everybody in the world, save
for my wife.

Acknowledgments

THE TITLE "WHAT'S WRONG WITH ME" IS A LINE FROM *The Graduate*.

Thanks to musicians whose music has inspired me for many years, whose lyrics may or may not have ended up in this book: Mudhoney, Pavement, Sebadoh, The Flaming Lips, Doug Shepard, The Replacements, R.E.M., Lisa Germano, Elliott Smith, Wilco, Sonic Youth, and Superchunk.

Thanks to those whose work inspires me: Lydia Davis, Susan Bernofsky and Christopher Middleton's beautiful translations of Robert Walser's prose and poetry, Robert Walser, Alice Munro, Joe Brainard, and Mary Ruefle.

Thanks to Todd McKinney, Erin Ergenbright, Van Wheeler, Matt Hart, Maggie Nelson, Jenny Boully, Melissa Ward, Kevin Sampsell, Elizabeth Johnson, Emily Schikora, Matthew Dickman, and Jesse Lichtenstein.

Thanks to Kevin McIlvoy, Tony Hoagland, Robert Boswell, and Antonya Nelson.

Thanks to Scott Nadelson and David Shields.

Thanks to Natalie Serber.

Thanks to Rhonda, Adam OR, and Liz at Hawthorne Books.

Thanks to Mom, Eric, Chris P, Dad, Susan, and Chris B. Thanks to Ally and Zach.

Thanks to Meg Roland and Perrin Kerns.

Thanks to the editors of magazines that published earlier versions of this prose:

172 | JAY PONTERI

David Shields from *Seattle Review* ("Putt-putt" and "The saddest part of the story")

Jenny Barber and Heather Madden from *Salamander* ("Listen to this").

Jonathan Fullmer from *Knee-Jerk Magazine* ("So hard it bleeds").

Thanks to Mary Coleman and Shari Levine. Special thanks to Dianne Stepp.

Thanks to Amy, for your forgiveness, for your beauty, for your love, the best gifts I shall ever receive.